"The authors have woven together a masterclass in personal transformation. Their step-by-step approach to embracing change, welcoming feedback, taking action, and holding oneself accountable is a pathway to extraordinary growth. If you are looking to unlock the full power of executive coaching and create a life of flourishing, this is a must-read."

—Dr. Tal Ben Shahar, cofounder of the Happiness Studies Academy; former Harvard University professor; internationally bestselling author

"Leadership is a journey of continuous learning, and *Becoming Coachable* is a valuable guide for that journey. The emphasis on creating flourishing environments is particularly timely and essential. It's a refreshing perspective that every leader should embrace."

—Sanyin Siang, #1 coach; Thinkers50 2019 inductee; author of *The Launch Book*

"This book is an invitation to open your mind, heart, and soul to the transformative power of coaching. It's a beacon of guidance in the vast sea of personal and professional development."

—Chip Conley, hospitality entrepreneur; *New York Times* bestselling author

"*Becoming Coachable* is a tour de force in the realm of leadership and personal development. Just as knowledge must be turned into action for companies to succeed, leaders must be open to the coaching process in order to truly flourish. This book is an exceptional guide to mastering coachability."

—Jeffrey Pfeffer, professor of organizational behavior, Stanford Graduate School of Business; coauthor of *The Knowing-Doing Gap*

"I've benefited tremendously from coaching and only regret not having started earlier. *Becoming Coachable* is a must-have transformative guide to personal growth that parallels the journey of building a successful business. I really enjoyed the practical approach to embracing change, feedback, action, and accountability. A highly recommended read for established and aspiring leaders alike."

—Alex Osterwalder, founder and CEO of Strategyzer; International Institute for Management Development visiting professor

"Coaching is one of the most powerful, transformative, growth-oriented methodologies that exists. Coaching empowers and creates possibilities beyond what seems possible. And yet, to fully benefit from professional coaching, one must be open to the process. The authors of *Becoming Coachable* have crafted an invaluable guide for growth through coaching, and provide a robust framework for those seeking to maximize the benefits of such an engagement. This book is a cornerstone for leadership development."

—Magdalena Nowicka Mook, CEO of International Coaching Federation

"*Becoming Coachable* presents the journey of executive coaching in an accessible and transformative manner. Just as we aim to revolutionize coaching delivery at Coaching.com, this book revolutionizes our understanding of the coaching process. It's a leadership development staple."

—Alex Pascal, founder and CEO of Coaching.com

"There is no greater factor to getting the most out of coaching than being willing to get the most out of coaching—and this book teaches you how! You don't have that many years in your career to make a real difference, so why not make as big a difference as you can, while you can? In these pages, Scott, Jacquelyn, and Marshall show you just how to get there."

—Brian O. Underhill, PhD, founder and CEO of CoachSource, LLC

1CO COACHES
—PUBLISHING—
AN IMPRINT OF AMPLIFY PUBLISHING GROUP

amplifypublishinggroup.com
publishing.100coaches.com

Becoming Coachable: Unleashing the Power of Executive Coaching to Transform Your Leadership and Life

The authors have tried to recreate events, locales, and conversations from their memories of them. In order to maintain anonymity in some instances, the authors have changed the names of individuals, their occupations, and places, and may have changed other identifying characteristics and details such as physical properties, circumstances, and places of residence.

For more information, please contact:
100 Coaches Publishing, an imprint of Amplify Publishing Group
620 Herndon Parkway, Suite 220
Herndon, VA 20170
info@amplifypublishing.com

Library of Congress Control Number: 2023909619

CPSIA Code: PRV0623A

ISBN-13: 978-1-63755-768-6

Printed in the United States

Here's to the coachable, who create collective prosperity that leads to human flourishing.

UNLEASHING THE POWER
OF **EXECUTIVE COACHING**
TO TRANSFORM YOUR
LEADERSHIP AND LIFE

BECOMING
COACHABLE

SCOTT OSMAN
JACQUELYN LANE
MARSHALL GOLDSMITH

CONTENTS

To the Reader xi

Foreword xiii

Introduction 1

PART ONE
THE BASICS OF COACHING

Chapter 1: On Coaching 13

Chapter 2: Before You Begin 41

Chapter 3: Getting Started 63

PART TWO
BECOMING COACHABLE

Chapter 4: Open to Change 87

Chapter 5: Open to Feedback 105

Chapter 6: Open to Taking Action 125

Chapter 7: Open to Accountability 141

PART THREE
TO WHAT END?

Chapter 8: Within You 165

Chapter 9: With Us 197

The Sources 217

About the Authors 225

Acknowledgments 227

Further Reading 239

Endnotes 243

TO THE READER

Even though leadership can be lonely, you do not have to be alone. And if you are willing to be open, coaching provides a world of support so that together we can create human flourishing. That may not mean much to you now, but we hope by the time you finish this book, it will. Soon, you will understand how important the work you do is and how, through executive coaching, your potential is unleashed and the lives of the people you love and lead are enriched.

Take a deep breath and let's begin.

With love, gratitude, and wonder,
Scott, Jacquelyn, and Marshall

FOREWORD

Let's say you spot a volume entitled *Becoming Coachable* in a bookstore. Immediately, you can think of a dozen people you know who should dive into its pages. If *they* read the book and thereby became better humans, your life would be easier, and the world would be a better place. People at the office, at home, in the airport—if only *they* could get coached, sweetness and light would be yours.

My friend Richard Branson of Virgin has a remarkably deft way of seducing ambitious people to become coachable. Having spawned more than 400 Virgin companies he finds himself in endless meetings, and yet always shows incredibly fresh enthusiasm each time. At the outset, he whips out a permanent-looking hardcover notebook and begins taking notes. He asks clarifying questions without sounding judgmental. What incredible shock value there is in doing that—the big boss is actually interested in your ideas! How often do leaders who matter to us most appear to be listening? It's not that he's agreeing to everything, but his willingness to engage is hugely motivating to others and even to Richard himself, as it helps him feel more present.

Wordlessly, Sir Richard is modeling what it means to be coachable. If a leader can ignite hearts and minds that way, then imagine what their team might think if they caught them with a copy of *Becoming Coachable*? What kind of message would you send, if spotted reading a copy?

Ironically, this is one of those cases where you really should make it about *you*, because only through your own vulnerable willingness to improve can you ever hope for others to have the courage to do so as well. My friends Curtis Martin and Pau Gasol lived this principle as superstars, earning them coveted spots in the NFL and NBA Halls of Fame, and they've continued to exercise humility even after reaching the pinnacle of their careers. This is what my colleague, Sarah Hirshland, CEO of the US Olympic Committee, and I often observe about athletes who become extraordinarily successful business professionals in their second careers. The best leaders are never above doing what they ask others to do.

In 1998, the World Economic Forum invited me to interview 200 leaders whose epic careers spanned decades, from Oprah and Quincy to Bill Gates and Bono, Nelson Mandela and the Dalai Lama. After two decades as a board member and senior executive, my adventure in Davos launched my second career—a CEO coach—along with a bestselling book, *Success Built to Last: Creating a Life that Matters*. Nelson Mandela insisted that I describe leadership as a commitment to coach others to discover their potential rather than focusing only on yours, to inspire people to own the collective journey as much as your own. You're only as good as the folks you can convince to come along.

Founder Charles Schwab built his company that way. Chuck recruited me to help create the first online investment firm,

Schwab.com. He was the dad I never had, always coaxing me to reach higher. "You will fail if you do not scale," he'd admonish. In other words, your job is to grow and help others grow or you will be left behind by nimbler competitors. To take your game to that next level, coaching is crucial.

During her career, Venus Williams had as many as four coaches at once, from experts in technique and conditioning to nutrition and mindset. Venus reminds me of two coauthors of this book, Jacquelyn Lane and Scott Osman, because they've got a great eye for finding exactly the right coaching talent for the right moment and purpose. Even when Venus turned to business, she could not imagine a world without a coach. She insisted that I join her in taking eight online Stanford classes to further beef up her formidable skills. She challenged me to become a better coach by applying the same obsession she had for excellence on the court, her incredible discipline and values as a human being, and her self-awareness and determination to transform from an individual superstar to a leader of teams. To say that she is coachable is an understatement.

Venus never rests on her laurels. Truly successful people never do. My Stanford professor Jim Collins opened one of his legendary bestsellers with a warning: "Good is the enemy of great." The road to greatness is never a static place where you've arrived as a high achiever. Growth is a practice, not a project.

For that reason, you deserve a great coach for every season of your career; a loving critic who holds you accountable yet withholds judgment. This volume's third coauthor, Marshall Goldsmith, calls me every day to check in like an older brother. We hold a half-hour ritual to update our goals, fitness, relationships, happiness, and meaning. It's shocking how much easier it is to give each other advice than to follow it! As Marshall once famously wrote, "What got you here won't get you there." To flourish means you're coachable about what really matters. Picking up this book is a step people will notice. When you grow, others follow.

Mark C. Thompson
Chairman, Chief Executive Alliance

INTRODUCTION:
A LETTER FROM SCOTT

I was not always coachable.

In 2014, I was introduced by a mutual friend to Marshall Goldsmith, a dynamic leader who is categorically recognized as the world's number one executive coach. At the time, I did not know anything about coaching. What's more, I certainly did not think I needed a coach. The introduction was simply an invitation pairing two people who tend to dream big. Marshall and I hit it off and were soon collaborating on some ideas for his now classic book, *Triggers*.

Not long after, he informed me that he had just taken Ayse Birsel's workshop, "Design the Life You Love," and had walked away with a powerful epiphany. Four of Marshall's heroes, Peter Drucker, Frances Hesselbein, Alan Mulally, and Paul Hersey had shaped his trajectory by being incredibly generous with their teaching, wisdom, and guidance. Marshall realized that a key aspect of designing his most fulfilling life would be to do the same for others. In that spirit, he decided that he would teach fifteen people everything he knew at no charge, with the only expectation being that they "pay it forward" and do the same for others.

He thought I could be helpful in making this vision a reality and that it would be an interesting experience for me. I agreed, and we decided to make it happen.

And then in a blur of activity, it all came into being. He posted a video on LinkedIn, and 12,000 people applied to be "adopted" by Marshall. Realizing the enthusiasm we had tapped into, we dutifully selected twenty-five people (ten more than we had originally planned) for what we thought would be a one-time event. But interest only increased, so we kept going. By the end of our first year, we had conducted four such sessions and built a community with a culture of giving back and teaching others. 100 Coaches was born.

Over the past eight years, the community has grown to more than 400 ("100" is now an expression of quality rather than quantity) and is a varied group of some of the world's most outstanding leaders, leadership thinkers, and leadership coaches. So here I was, at the helm of a coaching organization and constantly surrounded by the best in the field. And, surprisingly, I had never been coached.

By this point, I had changed my tune: I was no longer under the impression that I did not need a coach. In fact, I was actively seeking one.

In the early days, I asked various coaches if they would be willing to coach me, and invariably, due to their generous nature, all agreed. Each of the coaches asked a similar question: "What is the problem you want to work on?" The problem was this—I did not feel I had one. I was generally satisfied with my life, relationships, and work. I knew I needed to grow, but I didn't know how. The coaches found this puzzling and had difficulty coaching me. Instead, what nearly always happened was that I ended up coaching *them*. I naturally find myself wanting to be of service to the people around me, and my relationships with these coaches were no exception. During my first forays into being coached, I was fundamentally unclear on how to be on the receiving end, how to participate in the coaching process to get the care and support I needed.

The problem wasn't the coaches. It was me. I wasn't ready to be coached.

As the 100 Coaches Community expanded, I naturally began fielding requests from exceptional leaders for qualified coaches. Jacquelyn Lane and I met in 2020, and, together, we started designing and building the 100 Coaches Agency, focused on meticulously matching the right leaders with the right coaches.

The agency and our curated matching process quickly became integral to the 100 Coaches mission. Building a new company together and through our collaboration, I was developing as a leader. This journey required me to become open to change. As any good collaborator should do, Jacquelyn questioned why I or we did things a certain way and nudged me toward new habits. As I became more receptive to her input, I started to let go of strongly held beliefs about how we had to operate. I learned to be fearless. I learned to be open to taking action. And as I became open to taking action, I was willing to be held accountable for those actions.

This was the moment that I became coachable.

I finally understood the potential that could be unlocked through a transformation in my leadership and how a coach could support that evolution. Of course, the reason that Jacquelyn was nudging me to think differently was that we were growing and in demand, and I knew from Marshall's classic book that "what got me here won't get me there."[1]

So, I got a coach.

As the saying goes, the teacher appears when the pupil is ready, so too for me with my coach. Once I felt called to find a coach for myself, my friend Ayse (with whom I do the *Triggers*-inspired Daily Questions practice) recommended someone.

During our first conversation we explored working together, and he asked me what I wanted to work on. I said I didn't know what I wanted to work on and that I didn't know what I didn't know. I may not have realized it then, but my work with Jacquelyn had yielded a small yet profound change; the recognition that there was work to be done was the beginning of a larger shift. He recognized it and almost immediately replied, "Great, then let's work on expansion." That was the unlock I needed. Expansion was an idea I could get behind.

My coach served as a great mirror, helping me to see myself and others' perceptions of me more clearly. Our work enhanced my understanding of my leadership style and defined what was my most important work as a leader. It helped me become conscious of the way I live and lead and release the things that held me back. The process helped me elevate my thinking, to see beyond the day-to-day and to envision both where I and the company could go. During the next three months, the agency and I made great and swift strides.

My second coaching situation flowed from the first.

My first coach helped me name my aspiration. But what that looked like specifically and what it meant for the business was still missing. Now that I had experienced firsthand the transformative power of this work, I knew I wanted to explore where continued coaching could lead.

That's when I went looking for my next coach.

I subscribe to one of my favorite business thinkers' email news-letters. In one such newsletter, she wrote about her coaching work and had a link to sign up for a one-time coaching session. As a birthday present to myself, I signed up for a session as a chance to meet her and get a better understanding of her work. She asserts that by claiming one's own history, experiences, visions, and hopes, one can live more fully alive in the world. I wanted all of this. For me, yes, but also for my team and for our company.

I began the prework, and, during our back and forth, I resisted. I found myself uncomfortable because her input challenged my existing worldview. As anxious as I was about the work, I was also deeply respectful of the work's value. So, of course, I showed up.

And then I had an epiphany. By truly accepting her input, some important puzzle piece was falling into place. I was elated and knew that more epiphanies lay ahead. I took action and hired her as my ongoing coach. Through our work together, we came to understand that the same drivers and blocks that were impacting me were also affecting the business.

Through the steady nature of our coaching engagement, she assigned me different homework assignments and held me accountable. It was that process of keeping at it over time that kept me in the work. I gained clarity by taking small, yet inten-tional, actions. Each moment required something that I wasn't sure I had in me, but by keeping at it I found that I did. And the net result was liberating. Not just because I grew as a person, but also because I *learned* I could grow as a person.

It was the kind of coaching I needed to generate a new level of growth. My first coach helped me think differently, to see the world more expansively, to envision where I want to go.

My second coach helped me take this vision and put it into action, to focus my efforts, and to create robust systems for our business. And both experiences have taught me how to better lead and support others. Being coached has changed my life in innumerable ways. Coaching set me free.

I had been working on a book on coaching for more than a year. With the new insights, the collaboration with Jacquelyn and Marshall, and the support from my two coaches, the reason for the book became clear. Here I had been deep inside the world of coaching, had many friends who were coaches, and had access to the most remarkable talent in the world; yet, for the longest time, I did not know how to prepare for the journey. I did not know how to become coachable, and I suspected the same was true for many others.

That intrinsic gap in knowledge was the inspiration for *Becoming Coachable*. Marshall, Jacquelyn, and I wanted to write a book for anyone looking to grow in their leadership. This may include those who are "coach curious" and have wondered how the world of coaching works, whether or not they're already sure if it's right for them. We also wanted it to be a resource for those who are in the process of being coached but are looking for additional insight into how to make the most of the relationship. And we want it to be relevant for those who have been coached before, who may be looking for a deeper understanding of the transformational power of coaching and how to independently continue their development.

Coaching is one of the most important investments you will ever make in your life. It's an investment in your growth and future. It is a time and financial commitment, yes, but it yields an exponential return.

Most importantly, you only have a limited number of years in your career. The sooner you become coachable and find a great coach, the longer you will enjoy the benefits of coaching in your work and personal life.

Experience has taught us that when most people express interest in coaching, they really want to become better at their job, usually by becoming a better leader. What they find after being coached is that they are not *only* a better leader, but they have also become a better human being. Such transformation is pivotal to our collective human experience. It is a refrain to which we will return often in these pages.

This book answers the question of what it means to be coached. How is it performed? How do you prepare for it and ensure it is successful over time, from the start to the finish of the coaching engagement? This book is intended to demystify the process and illuminate the path to personal enlightenment by emphasizing the point of view of those being coached—i.e., the coachable.

This book is fundamentally about the power of relationship (namely, the coach-client relationship) to transform lives, so not surprisingly, it was born through relationships and collaboration.

Marshall, Jacquelyn, and I come from three different generations with varied life and career experiences that ultimately led us to executive coaching. Marshall has been a pioneer of executive coaching for forty years, and many of his methods and approaches are among the most widely used in the industry today. While, as a member of the millennial generation, Jacquelyn has had fewer years of professional experience, she has already established herself as an expert in the field of coaching through her work with some of the world's leading coaches. Her perspectives and intuition about people and coaching have proven invaluable in our work and the development and writing of this book. Each of us has coached and been coached many times, and our approaches and preferences vary.

The three of us are united in recognizing the contribution that coaching makes and are committed to the goal of helping you understand how to prepare for and get the most from coaching, both in your professional and personal life. We've seen firsthand the awe-inspiring transformation of too many executives to not be believers. This book has been a true collaboration and labor of love. While we each bring our unique experiences and stories to this work, we strove to find a voice that falls somewhere in between the three of us.

Jacquelyn and I run the 100 Coaches Agency, now considered the leading curator of executive coaching worldwide. After matching hundreds of coaches with clients, we recognize the patterns behind why some partnerships flourish and others fail.

In explaining the coaching process, we chose to practice what we preach. We looked first within ourselves at our own experiences before looking outwardly, just as a coachable leader must do. We talked to our colleagues in the 100 Coaches Community, and the over twenty coaches mentioned in this text have more than 400 years of combined experience in executive coaching. These are excellent coaches; we feel honored to have them as friends and collaborators. To avoid breaking narrative stride, they are simply name-checked in the text; we invite readers whose interest is piqued to flip to the back of the book, where we lay out an alphabetical list of these sources, each entry outlining their accomplishments.

Mentioning our pedigree of experience is not meant to strong-arm readers to accept our message. *Becoming Coachable* does not tell people what to do. Think of it more as *What to Expect When You're Expecting a Coach* (considered a title contender for a hot second). As a reader, you will use what you want to use and leave what you want to leave, safe in the understanding that this is your decision to make and journey to take.

In this book, we will cover three distinct, but not discrete, parts—they overlap and reinforce one another. The first three chapters, under the umbrella title "The Basics of Coaching," explore the world of coaching and its nuts and bolts. We will re-emphasize and expand upon many of the questions briefly evoked in the preceding paragraphs in part one. If you are already fairly familiar with the coaching process or have had an executive coach before, you may want to skim this section and head for part two.

The subsequent four chapters, grouped under the rubric "Becoming Coachable," focus on you, the coachable leader, and how you can prepare yourself to get the most benefit from the process. These chapters dive into what we call the "openness framework," which highlights the four key areas coachable leaders must remain receptive to in order to truly gain the most from their coaching experience.

The book's final part is perhaps the most intriguing and certainly the most unconventional. "To What End?" encourages you to think more expansively about what coaching can do for you and how it can transform your life and the lives of those you love and lead. The two chapters in this section detail the loftier long-term purpose of coaching and how growth can be sustained and expanded long after your coaching engagement has come to a close. It is here where we share our view of what is possible as a result of coaching and the potential you can seek for yourself. We will make the case for what we call Flourishing, an inclusive approach to business and life, by incorporating the lessons learned in the coaching engagement and expanding them beyond your immediate business environment. The lessons gleaned from coaching form a skill set that we believe can be transferred to others. A final informal section ends on a high note: a conversation among friends (you included) discussing Flourishing in action.

The observant reader may wonder if this is a self-help manual disguised as a business book. Perhaps. And we would hope you begin to understand, right now, that self-improvement is collective improvement, in business and in life. The gains made by successful executive coaching touch all corners of our lives. All business books (good ones, at least) abound with tales of personal struggle. You do not check your humanity at the office door in the morning, just as you should not leave lessons learned through coaching in your desk drawer in the evening.

We hope that *Becoming Coachable* answers fundamental questions about coaching. On its chronological journey from pre- to post-coaching, there will be several detours, some of which may amuse or disconcert, but all of which will edify.

Like me, you may not have always been coachable. But at the end of this passionate journey, you'll be ready to embark on the life-changing collaboration that is a coaching relationship.

Join us. We can't wait to see where this journey takes you.

Scott Osman
Cofounder and CEO, 100 Coaches

PART ONE

THE BASICS OF COACHING

CHAPTER ONE

ON COACHING

COACHABLE LEADERS

If you're reading this, we want to congratulate you. You've certainly worked hard to get to where you are today, and that's commendable. And if you picked up this book, that probably means you want to improve, grow, make more impact, and create an even better life for yourself and others. Thanks for being here; you are in the right place.

Coaching is one of the most powerful tools available to leaders today. Over the past few decades, coaching has evolved from something only practiced in the world of sports to a meta-skill employed in nearly every field and industry. There's something unique about the coaching method—a mix of skills practice, real-time feedback, advising, question-asking, psychology, and motivation—that makes it effective for growth in any area.

There has been much study and writing about the approaches of coaches, but we were surprised to find very little about the other side of the coaching equation—what it means to be coachable. Coachability, as we define it, is about the degree of preparedness a person has to get the most growth and development from the coaching process.

And we're not just talking about formal coaching engagements. If you're in a relationship with anyone who's invested in how you behave and lead, you are subject to some coaching. For example, you may have a spouse who wants you to put the cap back on the toothpaste tube. Or you have a peer at work who wants you to prioritize a certain project. Coaching is about embracing feedback to gain more perspective about yourself and how others view and experience you. And, if you are coachable, this perspective will help you grow into your best, fullest self.

While coaching does apply to these various relationships, this book will primarily discuss coaching in the context of a formal coaching engagement and how best to reap the benefits of such a collaboration. More specifically, and to the tune of our collective professional work, we focus on maximizing the efficacy of such an engagement in the high-achieving leadership space. The rewards of a successful coaching engagement are not only tangible and potent within one's career but extend far beyond office walls. Naturally, an executive coach will also open your eyes to how to respond to the other types of coaching and feedback presented in your life.

Between the three of us, we have witnessed hundreds of coaching engagements of all levels, industries, and challenges. When we sat down to really understand why some flourish and others fizzle, one major trend emerged—coachability. Leaders who go on to create the most impressive results in record time are the most coachable. An unprepared or unwilling client will likely meet with failure, no matter how dazzling their coach's track record. Becoming coachable is the cornerstone to success.

So, whether you already have a coach, are interested in hiring one, or simply want to learn and grow more as the result of the other people in your life who are (often unknowingly) offering you coaching and precious feedback, this book is for you.

The best place to start is to understand what kind of leader you are today. This will help you determine what kind of support you need from a coach and begin your engagement with eyes wide open. Coachable leaders come in many varieties; as many varieties, in fact, as there are businesspeople. While each person's needs and problems are unique, we want to highlight some common archetypes.

THE ESTEEMED EXECUTIVE

Coaches are masters at finding the code to unlock the most value from even the most formidable executives. When coach Carol Kauffman works with the most senior executives of an organization, she tells them she learned all she needed to know about leadership at age seven. That's when a friend shared the old joke about a 600-pound gorilla walking into a crowded bar. "Where does it sit?" goes the story. The answer: "Anywhere it wants."

When Carol tells that joke, leaders are often puzzled. "And...?" they want to know. "And," replies Carol, "you are the gorilla."

A skilled coach will help leaders uncover hidden truths about themselves—gorilla or otherwise—and how those truths sway their organizations. For example, Richard was the CEO of a bustling Fortune 100 retail company. Under Richard's command, the company grew rapidly, making him the envy of the business world. On the surface, everything seemed perfect. But beneath the surface, employees trembled in fear of their commanding and hard-charging leader, who was unaware of the counterproductive influence he had on the organization.

Despite the company's apparent success, there was a simmering undercurrent of dissatisfaction. Employees dreaded interacting with Richard, who frequently dismissed their ideas and suggestions without consideration. His abrasive demeanor stifled creativity and produced an atmosphere of fear and tension, with people tiptoeing around issues and avoiding confrontation. The company's innovation and growth began to stagnate.

Concerned that something was holding his organization back, Richard confided in a CEO peer who recommended engaging a coach. Richard sought out a highly skilled coach known for transforming good leaders into great ones.

The coach began by conducting anonymous interviews with employees to collect feedback on Richard's leadership style. The information gathered painted a picture of Richard's leadership that he had never seen before, revealing blind spots he had been oblivious to. With his coach's guidance, Richard embarked on a journey of self-discovery, learning the adverse consequences of his abrasive behavior and the importance of active listening, soliciting input, and fostering open communication.

The transformation was remarkable. As Richard's leadership evolved, so did the company culture. Employees became more engaged and motivated, the atmosphere shifted toward collaboration and innovation, and the company's performance skyrocketed.

Richard's example echoes many true stories of how a highly effective coach helped a top-of-the-ladder leader gain clarity— and, in turn, helped their organization soar.

Coaches talk a lot about unconscious biases or aspects of ourselves we don't see that get in the way of our growth. Writing in *Strategy+Business* in 2020, researchers at Merryck & Co and Barrett Values Centre described a study in which they compared self-assessments of 500 leaders with feedback from 10,000 of their peers and colleagues over a fifteen-year period. They found almost no overlap between what the two groups identified as areas in which the leaders needed to improve. In fact, in 80 percent of the assessments, all of the top three areas were different.[2]

We have all experienced a leader who appears to be blissfully unaware of their impact on others and how they are perceived. A closer look makes this situation seem predictable, perhaps unavoidable, as increased authority often results in decreased feedback due to real or perceived power dynamics.

For topmost corporate leaders, the most common failure, to see what is in front of their nose, may be called a paradox of leadership. Our coaches interviewed cite this paradox as pervasive. CEOs fail to recognize their own impact. If you are one such leader, the greatest problem with your leadership most likely derives from the fact that you are now a leader. "When you are the leader," says Alisa Cohn, "you don't realize that when you speak, you are standing on a table with a bullhorn, raining words down." At least some of the work you do with your coach will involve recalibrating employee impressions of you to a more human, less intimidating, scale.

The boss's questions are orders. His musings are orders. And his orders are orders. As Marshall says, the higher up you go, the more your suggestions become orders. Carlos thinks he's merely tossing an idea against the wall to see if it sticks. His employees think he's giving them a direct command. Carlos thinks he's running a democracy, with everyone allowed to voice their opinion. His employees think it's a monarchy, with Carlos as king. Upon your ascension to the highest level of business, the flow of feedback to which you had become accustomed as a mid-level executive can easily become a dribble that then may dry up altogether. Silence, crickets—this is often the result of the fear of executive power. A good coach, as we shall see here, has the tools to dissipate that fear and get valuable input flowing to you again.

THE PERSISTENT PATHFINDER

Another typical leader is someone in the middle to the top of an organization who is recognized as a high performer and major contributor. They are often given tricky projects and responsibility for large profits and losses but may lack the formal power or authority to effect change. They want to do more but are sometimes thwarted by the absence of a charter giving them the freedom to act, the nature of their title, and the power dynamics at play. Often, they are tasked with resolving seemingly intractable problems. They may even have trouble convincing colleagues that there is a problem at all.

These people do not command the deference shown to the C-suite, but they must somehow get on with the job, be it freeing a supersized cargo ship stranded in the Suez Canal or creating a serene chapel in the contentious conference room on the top floor. They must withstand the blow darts of criticism and lumber onward. A coach can help them with that.

An example: Katie, an executive who has been a director for some time, knows only too well the predicament. She has absorbed the revenue operations of the business inside and out, having first run channel sales, then channel strategy, and then sales operations. Her deep expertise in the ways things work means she is often called on to "help" with strategic things, to sit in on sessions in which she has no defined role. She doesn't have an official title that says she's in charge, but she is effectively making things happen all over the place. That's how she ends up being in a meeting where she spots something that is causing the business to flounder. She sees it clear as day. But not everyone else sees it. In fact, that's the problem. Every part of the business sees a sliver of the problem, but her interdisciplinary lens means she sees it more clearly.

Now Katie must figure out how to fix it. Because no one else sees it as clearly as she does, she has trouble mustering alignment from others. Plus, each party wants to blame someone else when there is no blame to be had. It's a gap, a space between every defined area that is causing the failure.

At first Katie wonders if she's tough enough to take on the challenge. But she knows that it needs a solution. And she knows she needs to learn how to drive a new approach that is some combination of strategy, operations, people alignment, and influence.

The business challenge demands her leadership—to charge into a thicket of issues. She knows she can't do this alone. That's where the coach comes in. Because she has a thinking partner— her coach—external to her organization, she has someone to turn to regarding this specific set of issues. And so, week by week, month by month, action by action, she doesn't become overwhelmed. Instead, she has a coach who judiciously helps her think through what the next right thing is, and, in so doing, Katie (and the business) power through the complex situation and reach the other side.

THE ACCELERATING INNOVATOR

Another creature of our coachable leadership differs substantially. Such a person is an ambitious visionary who wants to expand their hunting grounds at lightning speed. They also want to fix problems, and fix them fast. Often, they are entrepreneurs or founder CEOs.

One example is Etosha, an entrepreneur at a nonprofit who began her career working in health care. Then she received a seven-million-dollar grant from a philanthropy to start a venture fund to address Black maternal health. Black women in the United States are three times more likely to die from a pregnancy-related cause than are White women,[3] and Etosha has the charter to help address that disparity. She is ambitious and smart and needs to move quickly; her mission deserves it, and lives are at stake.

She had never run a high-growth organization. One of her first decisions was to enlist a cofounder who was a highly qualified expert in the space. Alas, the cofounder was going through personal issues and was not delivering in the way Etosha—and those who would be helped by their organization—needed him to. Etosha had to decide if the situation was fixable or if she needed to cut him loose. She had never faced such a decision before and had no idea how to approach the problem. She knew she could not afford to spend much of her time coaching and coaxing someone who should have been, in theory, as strong and competent as she was. However, they had already announced their partnership. So, what to do?

Etosha turned to her coach to help her work through this decision in an effective and efficient manner. Instead of the situation dragging on, she knew she would make the right call with the clarity of knowing she had thought it through well and with a sounding board.

Etosha and her coach put together a list of what would need to be true for her cofounder to stay on. It included both the "what" of the work but also the "how." Etosha did a first pass so she could think through each line item before her coach pushed and pulled on that list, making it more specific and measurable. In her coach, Etosha got the benefit of more than twenty years of business acumen—so she could solidify her thinking. That concrete list made it clear whether the cofounder was succeeding or not, and thus it made the decision of what to do next self-evident. This made her life easier; the issue was no longer about the cofounder but rather about answering the question: What does the firm need to meet its important mission? That was the revelation Etosha's coach was guiding her toward.

Our categorization of coachable leaders could go on and on. If you don't recognize yourself in the examples given above, not to worry. We've supplied these three profiles—the Esteemed Executive, Persistent Pathfinder, and Accelerating Innovator—only to underscore and exemplify the diversity of leaders seeking a coaching engagement. There are many, many others, but that would require a separate book, which is not our brief here. Regardless of your leadership level, style, or organization, coaching will help you better explore the professional world you inhabit. We expect that you will see yourself, somewhere, in the pages to come.

WHAT DOES IT MEAN TO BE COACHED?

People often ask us what it means to be coached. We have good news for you: If your boss or your board is retaining an executive coach for you, that means two things. One, that you have already laid down an impressive foundation as a leader. And two, that you have significant potential to develop further. Hiring a coach is among the surest investments a company can make in talent. The company's message: *When we envision our future, we see you there with us.* But there is another message as well: *Being an A-player and top performer does not mean you have, by default, made it.* Even if you are the CEO, you have room to improve. In fact, particularly if you are the CEO, your decisions exert influence across so many lives that operating with maximum effectiveness is not only desirable but also imperative.

The great news: Becoming the leader your company needs to meet the demands of your ever-expanding role can be among the most rewarding efforts of your career. The key word here is effort—you will need a lot. All the coaches we interviewed for this book state this clearly. You must put in the hard work. That should not be an insurmountable problem: We know you are accustomed to working hard, otherwise you would not be where you are. And if you are aspiring to get there, you probably rolled up your sleeves long ago.

So, you must clear away obstacles obstructing your path forward in the coaching process, whether they are mental, emotional, or social. Coaching is the deep-tissue massage of leadership development, applying the slow, steady pressure of self-inquiry, collegial candor, and consistent practice to examine faults and build transformative behaviors. It does not matter if your challenge at work is relatively minor, akin to a corporate stubbed toe, or devastatingly major, like a business train wreck. You should expect to feel discomfort while being coached. That's good. That means it is working. We, the authors, know this from experience: We've found that if feedback to us consists solely of sweetness and light, then there is trouble brewing.

You should be proud to have a coach. It means you have done well to get where you are and are committed to continuing your growth. Famed investor and businessman Warren Buffet said, "Generally speaking, investing in yourself is the best thing you can do." You are worth that investment.

Your coach is your guide, goad, whisperer, sounding board, thought partner, devil's advocate, confidant, and friend. They are devoted to your success and in it with you every step of the way. The relationship with your coach might well become among the most important in your life. Some leaders find those relationships so valuable that they extend them, in different forms, over decades.

Your coach will challenge you to hear things you do not want to hear and do things you do not want to do. They will suggest where to focus, but they will not drive their own agenda nor try to establish yours. Coach Prakash Raman offers the key advice to focus on the "one area you can make the greatest positive change." Your coach is aware that your time is limited and that your responsibilities may affect thousands of people and involve millions of dollars. Accordingly, they will endeavor to make your time maximally effective, prioritizing the things you consider most important and cocreating measurable actions, all while lending a compassionate ear.

Coaching works when you take it seriously and afford it the right level of attention. This is the success of you and your company that we are talking about, so the stakes are high. And what you learn can be lived beyond the coaching process. This is not business school, where you pack up your laptop at the end of class and leave the lecture hall. Although you will spend only an hour or so a week with your coach, you'll be engaging in difficult conversations, soliciting frank feedback, and exercising patience-straining degrees of self-discipline. The return on investment is clear: You will be learning how to be a better leader.

"Coaches work with smart, successful people," says Alisa Cohn. "The easy things, they have already done. The medium things, they have already done. The hard things, they have at least tried to do. What's left is the stuff they don't know how to do."

If you're lucky, transformations might arrive as epiphanies. A new perspective arrives in an instant or a mental model shifts overnight. When a coach helps you see something completely new, you may find new perspectives quickly. Even easily. Marshall observes that coaching works best with leaders who appreciate these transformational moments and also recognize that they do not last unless they are willing to put in the effort. Most importantly, you should recognize that a coach's primary responsibility is to always prioritize your interests and well-being.

Marshall was coaching Dr. Jim Yong Kim to support his growth as the president of Dartmouth College. Dr. Jim, as Marshall calls him, had grand plans to advance the influence and stature of the college by strengthening its position in health care and nurturing a student body that cared about issues like global poverty and inequality. Marshall supported Dr. Jim in understanding how to influence the competing and powerful factions at the college, including the board, the alumni, the faculty, and the students. Despite each constituency being critical to his success (and in turn, Dartmouth's success), each group believed it was most deserving of prioritization. While Dr. Jim's significant leadership contributions at Partners In Health and Harvard Medical School were impressive, this job undoubtedly was teaching Dr. Jim the art of compromise.

One day, Dr. Jim received a call from President Barack Obama asking him to consider the role of president of the World Bank Group. It was a perfect role for him, allowing him to continue to have an impact on a global scale and tackle systemic problems in ways that he was uniquely qualified. Dr. Jim struggled mightily with the decision; honoring commitments was core to his self-image, and he was entwined with Dartmouth at the time.

Coaching him, Marshall asked him what was more important to the world and to his values: helping this storied Ivy League institution advance or addressing the issue of global poverty? Marshall suggested that his exemplary contributions at Dartmouth would live on far after he departed the institution. But people living in poverty could not wait.

Marshall's words transformed Dr. Jim's thinking on the matter in an instant. Armed with this perspective, Dr. Jim made the difficult decision to leave the college he had come to love to answer the call of a lifetime. And answer he did: Dr. Jim became the twelfth president of the World Bank Group in 2012. His deft steering of the organization had major, real-world results—while he was at the helm, the global extreme poverty rate dropped from 13.2 percent in 2012 to 9.7 percent in 2017.[4] This is one example of many that illustrates the stark impression even one coachable leader can have on the world.

One of the rewards of being coached involves a neat twofold outcome. The qualities you need to be successfully coached—self-awareness, humility, the ability to listen, a hunger for feedback, a commitment to action, and a willingness to be held accountable—are precisely the qualities you need to lead. Becoming a good coaching subject is a way to prepare you for new, more demanding roles. "If you look at being coached as a chore, then you won't get much out of it," says Michelle Tillis Lederman. "You should look at your coach as a resource and a gift."

Not everyone is willing to be coached. If you are one in this minority, then don't waste your coach's expertise, your company's cash, and your own time. But if you are willing and eager to be coached, the insights are limitless.

WHAT MAKES EXECUTIVE COACHING DIFFERENT?

We love using the sports metaphor to describe coaching because it helps illustrate the dynamic relationship between coach and leader, much like the bond between a sports coach and an athlete united in a common goal. Starting in the mid-1800s, the word "coach" has been applied to people who prepare individual athletes and teams to compete.[5] Coaches have supplied the wattage that made stars like Wayne Gretzky, Kobe Bryant, and Venus Williams shine brightly. A coach's locker-room eloquence has become a staple of movies and television shows. Coaches labor to inspire the best of the best to get better. Can the same be said of business coaching? Recalling her college days as a varsity rower, coauthor Jacquelyn puts a finer point on the metaphor: No matter how naturally gifted an athlete, she says, if they are unwilling to be coached, they will not realize their potential.

Uncoached, Adonis will be left in the dust. As for those with God-given genius, many a barstool is now warmed by closed-minded could-have-beens.

In the early twentieth century, with the study of psychology and new technologies ascendant, versions of coaching left the sole arena of sports and migrated into organizations. Corporations increasingly viewed management as a science, comprised of universal principles by which executives could be trained. At the same time, individual leaders trumpeted their own visions and communication styles. Proto-business coaches, bearing titles like counselor or adviser, operated at a nexus of social science and art.

About forty years ago, coaching leapt across the sports and corporate moats to infiltrate wider society and culture. People in other walks of life began hiring personal coaches. Bill Clinton, Hugh Jackman, Oprah Winfrey, and even Metallica[6] have acknowledged the benefits they gained from coaching. Silicon Valley, where entrepreneurs must act as leaders from day one, is awash in coaches.

We focus in these pages on executive coaching, in which an expert coach—trained in psychology, experienced in business, or both—applies motivation, discovery, and discipline to help a leader develop self-awareness and make concrete progress toward career-centric goals. The relationship embraces complex nuance, influenced by the needs of the client, the desire of the boss, the approach of the coach, the culture of the organization, and the amenability of the leader's coworkers. But the underlying brief is straightforward: The coach is hired to prepare leaders to meet both their needs and those of their employer. On occasions when those needs conflict, the coach always remains in the leader's corner. This is paramount. Your coach's primary (if not only) mission is your success and fulfillment.

Coaching homes in on you as the student and as the subject of study. As you and your coach work together, he or she will develop a deep understanding of your character, aspirations, secret strengths, and emotional triggers. A coach will learn "about your longings, your fears, and your struggles," says Peter Bregman. "What do you want? What brings you joy? Where do you get stuck? You must show up with as much unbridled honesty as possible."

Another critical aspect that sets the executive coaching process apart: Much of it unfolds in something close to real time. Unlike other forms of development like therapy, it incorporates a very fast feedback loop, so you will know almost immediately whether something is working. Results of behavioral change are real and can be assessed with little lag time. And although you and your coach may meet just once a week, they will almost always be accessible to you within a reasonable time frame. That means you can discuss how to handle difficult situations just days or hours before you encounter them.

The effect of that immediacy can be powerful. One coach was sitting with Jeff, the CEO of a financial services firm, right before a major meeting. The coach asked Jeff to rate his levels of calm, clarity, curiosity, and compassion on a scale of zero to ten. Jeff gave himself tens on the first three but confessed that his compassion tank was low. The coach asked him to recall a moment with his son when he had experienced a ten-out-of-ten level of compassion. "I can do that," Jeff said.

In the subsequent meeting, a company executive announced that he was resigning to look after his dying father full time.

Then he started crying. "No one in the room knew what to do," recalls the coach. "Jeff got up out of his chair, sat next to the executive, put his arm around him, and said, 'We've got you.' Afterward, he told me he never would have done that if I hadn't asked him about compassion."

Finally, coaching involves not just you, but also those who work with you, care about you, and are invested in your success. Your coach is like the crew chief at a barn-raising, in which you are the barn. With the help of your boss and colleagues, you will address the right issues. Also with their help, once you've resolved those issues, the changes will stick.

Sustainable, long-term change does not happen in isolation. You cannot do this by yourself. None of us can. We need the humility to recognize that.

WHEN YOU NEED A COACH

Let's be clear up front. Coaching is most effective when we work with successful executives who want to be as impactful as they can be. Why? Because they are usually interested in being their best and recognize that they cannot do that alone. We know that executive coaching targets people within organizations who have vision and the broad authority to execute on it. That includes C-suite denizens, presidents, vice presidents, directors, division leaders, and the most promising high potentials. Those leaders' decisions create jobs, drive economic growth, introduce innovations, and have the power to do great good. Alternatively, if weaknesses persist unchecked, they can inflict great damage. As an example, many of us have worked with leaders who unintentionally stall an organization's progress because of slow decision-making as a result of trying to understand everyone's viewpoint. A laudable instinct, yet these sorts of shortcomings exist everywhere for all of us but are especially pernicious for those with authority.

Li, a technology executive, was one such leader. He insisted that every major decision be made by team consensus, a difficult requirement for an organization composed primarily of opinionated product engineers. In the absence of consensus, he continued to ask for increasing amounts of data, never quite sure he had enough information to make a decision. The delay wreaked havoc in his organization: Everyone knew that they needed to keep moving forward to meet their ambitious goals, but without their leader's buy-in, how could they act?

Li's coach helped him realize that not making a decision was also a decision and had real consequences, both for the company and for morale on his team. His coach told him about a process employed by one of his professional role models, Jeff Bezos, who categorizes decisions as either reversible or irreversible.[7] If decisions are reversible, make a decision very quickly based on limited data and gut instinct. And because the decision is either partially or fully reversible, if additional data and testing reveal that it doesn't work, make a shift. If irreversible, be more thoughtful and take a bit more time, but still give yourself a deadline to make the final decision. While there were still occasionally those who dissented, overall, Li's team was happy to have him be the tiebreaker and provide a clear direction. Together with his coach, Li established a culture where his team could disagree and debate an idea, but ultimately all would commit to the eventual final decision.

The success of executives matters hugely both to direct stake-holders and to the far broader public indirectly affected by their performance. The executive's happiness matters as well, to the companies that employ them, their colleagues, their families, and, of course, themselves.

Leaders may seek executive coaching at any time. Typically, we find a coaching engagement coincides with an organizational or personal inflection point. The board may be working on a succession plan. The coach-curious executive may be preparing to assume new responsibilities, such as head of a global division or leadership of a large and fractious team. The company may be undergoing drastic change: grappling with a disruptive technology, facing a formidable new competitor, or experiencing discord after a merger.

Or the trigger may be psychological. The leader feels burned out, overwhelmed, or dissatisfied. Operating at the apex of the company pyramid, the executive suffers from isolation and needs someone to help them weigh priorities and reframe vexing questions. Perhaps stress is degrading their physical health and dealings with others. In her book *In Your Power: React Less, Regain Control, Raise Others*, Sharon Melnick presents a new approach for all leaders to stop reacting to others' limitations and instead raise themselves and others to be limitless.

Coaching endows the leader with the strength and resilience to weather most storms. Stephanie, an executive at a marketing firm, noticed that the company culture was unsupportive of women. After seeing too many of her female colleagues heading out the door, Stephanie hired Sharon as her coach. Stephanie had already tried discussing the problem with the company's owners, three older men. "Their vague response felt like they had given her a pat on the head and sent her away," says Sharon. "She didn't know whether to stay or leave."

Working with her coach, Stephanie started shaping the culture herself, building relationships with the board and enlisting the support of other women executives. She persuaded the owners to reduce their share of the firm by 25 percent and distribute the equity to their highest revenue producers, all of whom were women. The firm's results were off the charts. "The owners were so impressed that they made her CEO," says Sharon. "She told me the best part was when younger women in the firm came up and thanked her."

Even if you are in a great place professionally, mentally, and emotionally, with coaching you will start to think more expansively about yourself, your career, your company, and your life. Your coach can help you dream bigger and realize those dreams. Invariably, you will find yourself in a better place, perhaps far better than you could have imagined.

MISCONCEPTIONS ABOUT COACHING

By this point you may be wondering if we are directing you to therapy. No. A coach and a therapist are different—and we'll explain why later. For now, think of a coach as an incredibly powerful way to change the effectiveness of leaders and the lives of those they lead. People generally don't think much about coaching until they reach new professional heights. Consequently, some harbor misconceptions about how it works and what it is meant to do. Here, we'd like to debunk a few coaching myths.

HAVING A COACH IS SOMETHING TO BE ASHAMED OF.

Forty years ago, coaching may have been seen as a remedial exercise or a sign of weakness, but that is no longer the case. Today, having an executive coach to support your growth can be seen as a badge of honor. If anything, you must resist the temptation to parade your coach around the office like a gleaming advantage. Companies typically invest in top-tier executive coaches for their most consequential and promising leaders. That does not mean your coach won't explore your weaknesses and help hold you accountable. But having a coach should be something you are proud of. Only, try to be modest about it.

HAVING A COACH MEANS SOMETHING IS WRONG WITH YOU.

Everyone has flaws. There is no shame in that. For leaders, the veneer of omniscience expected in the past now seems a laughable proposition. Leaders today know they are expected to be human. When subordinates see their boss working with a coach to strengthen active listening skills, apply new design thinking models, or manage their frustration, they view that as a sign of respect for them and authentic concern for their well-being.

The most effective coaching fosters growth. You don't just want to eliminate those barriers to advancement erected by your situation. You want to eliminate the barriers you place on your own potential when you tell yourself, "If I could just get to this place, then that would be enough." Coaching encourages you to expand your possibilities.

THE COACH IS THERE TO FIX YOU.

Coaching is more like physical therapy than surgery. You meet with a physical therapist on a regular schedule. During those sessions, you work together to improve things like strength and range of motion. Then you go home and do the exercises yourself, over and over, for however long it takes. The physical therapist doesn't fix you. You fix you. The therapist shows you how and keeps you accountable. Coaching works the same way.

It is not a perfect analogy, though. Both physical therapy and coaching treat pain and build strength, yes. But the challenges a coach helps "treat" are far less defined. You are frustrated in your job; you feel you have untapped talents; you want to contribute more but don't know how. A physical therapist knows which tendon you have injured and exactly how to heal it. You and your coach, however, must explore your pain points and dive deep to achieve that level of clarity.

MENTORS DO THE SAME THING AS A COACH, AND THEY DO IT FOR FREE.

Mentors are wonderful. They can advise and guide you, usually based on their own experiences. We always recommend having one or two functional mentors who can assist you on your journey. Whereas a coach is knowledgeable in human behavior and leadership, a functional mentor has extensive experience and knowledge in their field. More often, mentoring is about providing career direction based on the mentor's lived experience and possibly about opening doors as you pave your own way. A mentor may offer suggestions, but it is ultimately the mentee who will need to navigate and implement these suggestions at will. A relationship with a mentor is generally voluntary, based on goodwill and mutual respect. That said, a mentor is generally not paid for their work and will have responsibilities outside mentorship, so they may not be open to being leaned upon too heavily for support. That's to be expected in most scenarios.

The job of the coach is different. The coach focuses on specific goals or skill sets to improve an individual's performance and leadership abilities within an organization. Coaching is a proactive engagement from both sides and helps you find ways to shift your perspective and build new mental models. Many coaches have professional certifications and training in coaching methodologies or techniques, which they apply as appropriate to help their client achieve their objectives. An experienced coach, having worked with scores of executives, usually addresses your growth and development from their extensive coaching experience rather than from personal lived experience. Yes, an executive coach is usually hired by a company or individual, but that also means that it is their job to support you. They are available for you as needed, and their sole objective is your success.

HAVING A COACH IS LIKE SEEING A THERAPIST.

It is important to note that there may be some overlap between executive coaching and psychotherapy, as both fields can incorporate elements of the other to support clients more effectively. However, the primary distinction lies in the context, focus, and goals of each approach. In other words: The similarities are minimal, and the distinctions abound.

Coaching primarily focuses on how the executive can improve their leadership performance, career development, and goal achievement within the context of an enterprise. Therapy's purpose is broader and focuses on addressing mental health issues, relationship challenges, or life transitions to improve well-being. While its benefits can extend beyond the office, executive coaching is primarily about and for your career. We spend a huge percentage of our lives at work, so it makes sense to have a coach who can understand both your personal challenges and have a deep business background and acumen. Your coach will often meet with your team and other people you work with (called your stakeholders), whereas a therapist will not. Coaching engages the organization. Therapy is usually invisible to the organization.

Coaching and therapy share similar blueprints. The coach or psychologist guarantees confidentiality. In return, the client or patient commits to absolute candor. Coaching and therapy address how we process our purpose and assign meaning to the events of our lives. But therapy digs deeper into psychological motivations, possibly including elements of trauma; it helps patients explore their feelings and understand why they do what they do. Coaches also help leaders become self-aware but are often more concerned with rapid, pragmatic, measurable change specific to the leader's performance within their role in the organization.

It is important to note that psychotherapists, including psychologists, psychiatrists, clinical social workers, and counselors, are licensed mental health professionals who have completed extensive education and training in various therapeutic modalities. Coaches are not a replacement for counseling or therapy, especially if diagnosed mental health issues are at play. If you are unsure about whether coaching or therapy is right for you, please consult a medical professional.

YOUR COACH SHOULD HAVE
WALKED IN YOUR SHOES.

This is a very common misconception, and we understand why. Seeking out a coach with experiences as close as possible to our own to ensure the coach can speak our specific career language is a very natural instinct. But unless your chief objective is acquiring a thought partner on business issues, a consultant who can provide topic-area input, or a kibitzing partner to share insider industry gossip, there really is no advantage to hiring someone who has done what you do (not to mention, due to rapidly changing social, technological, and economic conditions, one's previous experience becomes quickly outdated). Most coaching involves identifying weak spots, changing behaviors, and reimagining goals—none of which carries an overlapping, specific industry prerequisite. Coaches with a variety of business experiences, meanwhile, can expose you to best practices from roles and sectors with which you may not be familiar.

ALL COACHES ARE GOOD.

Our hope is that the vast majority of coaches have high ethical standards and are truly "good" at their core. But are all coaches good at what they do? That's a different question altogether.

Like many similar industries, coaches exist at all experience levels, from beginners through super-elite coaches with decades of experience. At each experience level, you have a certain break-down of quality: There are good coaches, and there are great coaches. There are natural talents and those who have worked their tails off. There are "ol' reliables" and those with star power. And in that mix, we have to consider that there are also—yes, we'll say it—bad coaches. They usually don't last very long.

A bad coach may masquerade as a good coach at first. But, *only* at first. Coaching is a results-driven business. And not only will the leader quickly realize their coach doesn't have the tools or training to deliver on their promises, their organization will see it, too. In even more damaging scenarios, a bad coach may actively provide harmful advice or compromise anonymity of stakeholders participating in initial assessments, though we certainly hope this is rare.

We must highlight the marked distinction between experience and quality. Should a beginner coach jump in by coaching a CEO of a Fortune 500 company? No, certainly not. Does that mean they aren't a great coach for a leader starting out in their career? Not at all. All coaches start somewhere. The good ones are the ones who have the capacity to thrive and help their clients thrive.

There is also a marked distinction between a poor coach-leader match and quality of coach. The coaching partnerships that succeed are the ones in which the coach and leader deeply respect and understand each other's working styles. A bad match doesn't mean a bad coach.

The coaching industry is not immune to oversaturation. And with oversaturation comes a need to weed out low-quality coaches who lack the skills, qualifications, and experience to truly transform you and your leadership.

It should be noted that the benefits received from coaching discussed in this book assume a high-performing coach is in the mix. In chapter two, we touch on the different pathways to finding such a coach and share some of the finer details you may want to discuss with potential coaches.

Misconceptions aside, coaching is one of the most powerful

tools available today for personal and professional transformation. Your coach can help you achieve great things, both in your career and in your life. "When I coach people," says Peter Bregman, "I am coaching them to be exceptional leaders *and* stellar human beings."

Key Coaching and Leadership Concepts

In this chapter, we've shared some foundational theories and myths about coaching. This groundwork should help you understand that obtaining a coach is a positive opportunity for unparalleled growth.

- **Learn your coaching type.** There are many types of coachable leaders. Before entering a coaching engagement, spend some time determining what type of client you are and ways in which a coach could support you.
- **See your blind spots.** Arguably, the most common challenge among leaders is their ability to understand their impact on the organization and how they are perceived by others. A coach can help you collect valuable feedback and identify key areas for development.
- **Know what it takes to lead.** The qualities you need to be successfully coached—self-awareness, humility, the ability to listen, a hunger for feedback, a commitment to action, and a willingness to be held accountable—are precisely the qualities you need to lead.
- **Look to sports coaching for a frame of reference.** Be it athletics or leadership, top performers know that they cannot

do it alone and recognize coachability as a key differentiator. Like with sports coaches, an executive coach will examine your innermost strengths, motivations, and weaknesses to encourage peak performance.

- **Be aware of your own inflection points.** Coaching engagements often coincide with an organizational or personal inflection point. The coach-curious executive may be preparing to assume new responsibilities, or the company may be undergoing change. Personal crises also trigger the need for coaching: The leader may feel burned out, overwhelmed, or dissatisfied.

- **Break through common misconceptions about coaching.** There are a variety of coaching myths that you should throw right out: Having a coach is something to be ashamed of; having a coach means something is wrong with you; the coach is there to fix you; having a coach is like seeing a therapist; a mentor can do the coach's job; a coach needs to have held a similar role as you; all coaches are created equal.

- **Understand who executive coaches are and what they can do for you.** An executive coach will have an understanding of psychology and business. They deal with the whole person with an emphasis on delivering business and personal results. A coach will likely involve your team or other key stakeholders in the process. A coach should always prioritize your interests and well-being. The relationship with your coach might become among the most important in your life.

Hiring an executive coach is an investment in your future as a leader. Your coach will help you remove barriers that stand in the path of realizing your potential.

CHAPTER TWO

BEFORE YOU BEGIN

CHOOSING YOUR COACH

We understand that the process of finding a coach—the right coach—may be daunting. But do not let this stop you. The view is worth the climb. And there are companies and resources that exist to help you along the way.

There are three common methods to finding a coach: searching for one on your own, taking recommendations from a trusted colleague or businessperson, and using a reputable agency. Some are fast and easy, while others take time but can yield a more meaningful collaboration. There isn't one right way to find a coach—what matters is that you find the right one for *you* who will help you and your organization move mountains.

If you start with an Internet search by typing "executive coach" into a search engine, be prepared for the deluge. Even after you've winnowed out the ads for luxury bus services and the like, tens of thousands of entries for coaching services remain. As with the results of most Internet searches, many of the listings are junk. Of course, some aren't, and you could find a valuable and transformative coach in this manner—but it will take some time and effort to get there.

Requiring certification of a prospective coach doesn't help much in your search, either. John Reed, who wrote *Pinpointing Excellence: Succeed with Great Executive Coaching and Steer Clear of the Rest,* estimates that there are between 600 and 1,000 programs worldwide that provide some kind of coaching certification, many as unreliable as the individuals seeking their seals of approval. "You don't want to jump in the boat with a marginal player or a fraud," he says. "The number of clients mistakenly hiring coaches certified by less established programs is stunning."

Others start their coaching search by going to their colleagues and peers. The "I know a guy" school of hiring could yield quality candidates—particularly if the recommendation comes from a leader operating at a similar level as you. However, keep in mind your own idiosyncrasies—as we've mentioned before, a coach who's right for one person may not be right for another, regardless of their overall success and experience.

In either case, you must do your research into the background, training, experience, and methods of any coach you interview. You should consider only candidates with verifiable records of success working with executives. Regardless of whether you find your coach on your own or via an agency, it's important to ensure you are considering facets of not only what the coach has accomplished in their lifetime, but also *who they are.* It's this relationship-first focus that can make all the difference in identifying the right coach.

Executive coaches can be academics, clinicians, entrepreneurs, former executives, or career coaches. Coaches may be broad in their approach or specialize in specific areas. For example, a former broadcaster may specialize in coaching leaders on communication and executive presence. But most come from one of two backgrounds. Some are psychologists and social scientists with deep knowledge of human behavior and how to help people change. Others are veterans of the business world, chiefly former executives with first-hand experience of the leadership growing pains their clients endure. Some have been coaching professionally for decades. Others have just recently emerged from executive suites.

In coaching, business and behavior are inextricable. Consequently, the best coaches combine elements from both areas, addressing a wide range of business and leadership challenges. Great coaches from the business world are well-versed in both human and organizational behavior. Those with a psychology background are experts in behavior. But many know a lot about business from their years coaching leaders and, often, from previous careers.

The relationship between leader and coach combines the personal with the professional. There needs to be a complicity between the two of you. You both must feel a connection that embodies ease of communication, instinctive understanding, respect, and trust. You must be comfortable in one another's company.

That doesn't mean you must have a lot in common. You are looking for the person most likely to get results for you and from you. Perhaps you prefer someone who is similar to you in personality or career path because you feel a natural rapport and kinship. Yet choosing somebody different from you may broaden your perspective and help you embrace behaviors that are not in your normal repertoire.

All coaches will both support and challenge you. But the degree to which they do one versus the other varies as well. Some coaches are gentle and nurturing. If you are worried that you'll be devastated by your colleagues' feedback, for example, you might want someone who makes a point of measuring bad news against the good. Alternatively, you might work better with a person akin to a drill sergeant who challenges you and tests your limits. In that case, make sure you're ready and willing to take what they dish out. After all, you'll be talking about your life and leadership. It can get personal. "Everyone who thinks they want a coach says, 'I want to be challenged. I am okay with tough love,'" says Caroline Webb. "But it is harder than many people think when it starts to happen."

For example, consider Suzy from a major financial services company. She said she was ready to hear the full truth. But when push came to shove, she was surprised how much it stung to hear that her team was frustrated with her leadership. Her coach asked how she felt, and the reality was that she was blindsided. Suzy had been blissfully unaware of her team's thoughts on her leadership; now, it was staring her in the face. She felt embarrassed at her lack of self-awareness, much like realizing that she had a remnant from her lunch salad in her teeth all afternoon. Her coach reminded her that it was more embarrassing to pretend it wasn't there and to go about things as she always had, rather than taking the more mature (but more difficult) route of listening to and addressing the feedback her team had generously provided.

Regardless of your coach's style, you will have to put in some effort to identify them—whichever way you go about it. Thus far, we've covered two avenues that have yielded many strong coaching partnerships, though they rely heavily on a combination of diligence and connections. This brings us to the third method of finding a coach: through a reputable agency.

Finding a coach through an agency takes some guesswork out of whether the match will be successful. Though not a guarantee (few things in life are), an agency with a proven track record can help provide a curated, thoughtful approach to the matching process. To put it bluntly: This saves you time and resources.

Each agency has a different approach to pairing prospective coaches with clients, some more involved than others. Below, we outline our curated process of matching coaches and leaders at the 100 Coaches Agency, in hopes of helping you feel confident in your coach selection, regardless of the method you use to find them.

FIRST: THE INTERVIEW

We start by interviewing the leader—challenges noted, temperament assessed, and goals outlined. This is one of the first dedicated times that we're getting to know who you are as a leader, why you want a coach, what you stand to gain, and how our work together could change the world.

SECOND: CANDIDATE ASSESSMENT

Based on the initial interview, we look into our network of executive coaches and recommend those most suited to your needs by assessing potential coaches' prior experiences in addressing the leader's primary challenges, work history, and relevant training. We evaluate logistics such as time zones and desired availability. And most importantly, we prioritize the personalities of the coach and client and how they fit together. In the end, we hope to facilitate a strong, trusted bond—and for that to happen, to some degree their personalities will need to mesh.

Whether you're finding your coach on your own or working with an agency, we recommend identifying or requesting to interview three candidates who could be your coach. Similar to buying a house, you want to explore options to begin to get a feel for what works for you and what does not. Gaining familiarity for the territory, for your likes and dislikes, can only be known through multiple conversations. (Be wary of too many conversations, however. They can start to run together or cause "analysis paralysis.")

THIRD: THE CHEMISTRY CALLS

Soon after the initial interview and assessment periods, we guide you to conduct what we call "chemistry calls" with those we recommend, usually via video calls. You need not prepare for these calls (unless you want to). The conversation should flow naturally, and a skilled coach will guide the encounter as needed. During these introductory conversations, you should get a sense of how coaches prefer to work and what they will expect from you. Some questions you pose to them—about subjects like their motivations, openness to outside ideas, and strengths and weaknesses—might be similar to the questions the coach will pose to you at the start of an engagement. Take the opportunity to explain your own goals and preferences, and these conversations should help you further clarify them.

Make sure to cover all the bases. Do not worry about straying to subjects that don't relate directly to your job or to the coaching. A coach works with the whole person. You will both be more comfortable if neither of you is a closed book.

If things really click, then the conversation will bloom. You'll enjoy getting to know one another. Both you and the coach should come away with a clear idea of what working together will look and feel like. Some of that will change as the coaching progresses. But when you sit down for your launch meeting, you shouldn't feel like strangers.

"Look for radically different backgrounds and philosophies," says David Noble. "You need data points. Don't just go with the first coach you talk to." We recommend speaking to three coaches at a minimum so that you better understand the coaching landscape and feel like you can make an informed decision. If all else fails, we recommend trusting your instincts. Only you can say what is best for you.

Even if you (and the agency, if one is involved) do everything right, coach-leader mismatches occasionally occur. "If you don't feel like you are learning anything, and when you see your coach's name in your calendar your energy goes down, that is probably not the right coach for you," says Carol Kauffman. If that happens, don't tough it out for six months. A better fit is out there and won't be hard to find. And once you find the right coach for you—even if the revelations are difficult, even if there is work to be done—we promise, you will enjoy and be grateful for the process.

A COACHING PRIMER

Let's think a bit about the actual experience of coaching. What does it feel like? Well, it is a relationship, so every coaching session will reflect the dynamic of two high-powered personalities. The goal of the coaching relationship is your growth and development, so you'll want to make sure to put your needs first and incorporate the elements that work for you. For example, perhaps you prefer to meet less frequently but for a longer amount of time: In this case, you'd request that a coach accommodate two-hour, rather than one-hour, meetings. Make sure to voice your opinions and needs, regardless of the circumstance or prevalence of your request in the larger coaching world. With that in mind, in this section we explore themes and elements common to coaching engagements, so you have a baseline framework of what to expect.

DURATION

Most engagements start with a six-month minimum term. Six months is about how long it will take you and those around you to start seeing measurable results. If you and your coach both consider the engagement valuable and productive, then you can extend it. That happens frequently.

Some coaches cap engagement length at around a year. Others will work with you for the better part of a decade. In those latter cases, you and your coach typically will have accomplished the bulk of your goals in the first year or two. By that time, you will have come to rely on your coach as a trusted sounding board and an indispensable member of your informal team of advisors. In many cases, you will end up friends.

Or you and your coach may part ways at the end of one engagement only to join forces again as you face fresh challenges. Another promotion. A new job. A market disruption. A boss brought in over you to shake things up. Likely, you will stay in touch between gigs for spot questions or a little maintenance work. There may or may not be a fee for those services, depending on you and your coach's relationship.

Alternatively, you may hire another coach, at some point, to handle new challenges and introduce you to different ways of looking at your world. There is a cascading effect to human development. The way leaders use coaches echoes that.

TIME

As a rule of thumb, you and your coach will meet at a predetermined time for one hour every week or for one to two hours every other week. You are expected to commit to the schedule. In addition, coaches usually make themselves available between regular meetings by email, text, or phone. Because coaching unfolds concurrently with the work you're being coached for, you can consult the coach if a particularly nasty challenge surfaces at a time when you are not scheduled to sit down together. Or you may want to get their read on an emerging situation or report a triumph or a disappointment.

Your commitment to the schedule will reflect your commitment to the work. Investing your time and effort will yield lifelong returns. But not everyone is willing to do the work. Many of the coaches we interviewed told stories of clients blowing off weekly appointments, claiming busyness and other priorities. They may not last long as clients and certainly do not reap the full benefits of coaching. Coaching requires you to work on yourself outside of the weekly rendezvous. If you do not do the homework or practice your targeted new behaviors, then the coach cannot help you and may not want to waste time trying. "In my contracts, there is a clause that says if two months in a row you don't do your work, then the contract is over and you forfeit your investment," says one coach, who estimates she lets go of 10 percent of her clients. "If you don't want to do it, then there is no hounding by me that will make you. You need to be able to do the work with me so that you know you will maintain it for the long term after our work together is complete."

VENUE

More than 80 percent of coaching today takes place via video-conference. That was true even before the COVID-19 pandemic caused us to begin working remotely en masse. A coach may want to observe you in person in your professional environment, and you may want that as well. Or you might arrange for the coach to visit every few months and work with you and your team together. Keep in mind that if you prioritize in-person interactions, then that limits your choice of coach to one who works in your area or is willing to travel frequently. Most leader-coach pairs are satisfied with remote interactions.

INVESTMENT

A coach's fee should be directly proportional to the leader's risk/reward outcome, and it can vary depending on the coach's experience level, scope of work, the leader's level of impact on the organization, and the organization's impact on the world. In short: If the stakes are higher, the fees are higher (and are earned through measurable outcomes, another reason you'll want to have a reputable coach with a track record of success).

At the time of this writing, some Fortune 500 companies may pay tens of thousands of dollars a month (and up) to get elite coaching for their CEOs, reflecting the extraordinary value those executives create by becoming better leaders. Coaches just getting their start are likely to charge less, providing great value to those looking to benefit from coaching on a budget. Mid-level executives or established entrepreneurs at smaller companies may have the bandwidth to invest in the wide-ranging middle ground. All this said, estimated fee ranges are only one piece of the puzzle. A quality coach who is prepared to assume the level of responsibility and stakes required by the coachable leader will always deliver value, regardless of the financial investment on the table.

A study by MetrixGlobal, commissioned by a Fortune 500 company, backs this up. The study found a 529 percent financial return on investment from coaching, in addition to intangible benefits. When employee retention attributed to better leadership is thrown into the mix, that number rises to 788 percent.[8] Some studies have reported even higher returns.

Whether you agree with these studies or not, improved leadership strongly benefits organizations financially. When people or organizations make traditional investments, they are usually thrilled by 20 percent returns. If you had even a small chance of making a 50 percent or 100 percent return, wouldn't it be worth it? Often, high-reward investments come with high risks. The unexpected factor about coaching is that the risks are very low. If a leader truly commits to being coached, and the onboarded coach has a proven track record of success, it will work. It's at least worth giving it a shot.

Many coaches bill monthly or quarterly rather than hourly. That should make you comfortable using your coach's services as much as you need. If circumstances emerge that require frequent consultations, then you don't have to worry about the meter running.

Considering the financial investment and weighing it against the stakes at hand is an important step in the process. Keep in mind: Your investment of candor, commitment, openness, and caring will be just as great. In the words of Warren Buffet: *You are the investment.*

ARE YOU A JERK?

Okay, we admit it. On occasion, each of us has been a jerk—personally, professionally, or sometimes both. In fact, being a jerk is so prevalent that every so often it is important to admit it and forgive ourselves. While we admit to being jerks from time to time, let's also focus on the main goal of this book: We want to overcome our negative tendencies and improve. Coaching can help us get there.

There is a myth that leaders are supposed to be flawless, but we believe it's important to acknowledge the humanity in all of us. By virtue of being human, all leaders have imperfections. No one is without shortcomings that can translate into off-putting behavior. Maybe you're prone to interrupting others. Maybe you unknowingly still harbor some gender bias. Although barefaced sexism and racism have lost many of their adherents, atavisms are still lurking out there, capable of demoralizing and demotivating a good number of people in the workforce. Or maybe you're a generation warrior who discounts the contribution of younger colleagues, dismissing them as whippersnappers who should put a lid on it until they have paid their dues. Or perhaps you tell jokes that some deem insensitive or offensive. Whatever the flaw, and there are many possible other ones, the potential to come across as a jerk never really dims—until that flaw is addressed. Coaching can help there—not only in identifying the flaw, which is an imperative step, but in correcting it, holistically and in a way that resonates with others. (And to be clear, we're not making excuses for damaging behavior. Real growth and positive change can't begin without a leader first acknowledging the need for improvement.)

Nobody wants to see that someone has covertly placed on their desk a book with the title *Work Jerks* or *Toxic Boss*. Perhaps you know you can be a challenging boss when poor business results make you frustrated and test your ability to control your temper. Or you carry stressors from other parts of your life into work. That was the situation for Amanda, a senior leader at an investment bank, who had gained a reputation as a screamer. She told her coach that she had a problem with her children. When things were bad at home, "she acted out inappropriately, which she sometimes was aware of and sometimes not," says the coach. Amanda said she couldn't help herself, which did not fly with her coach. "My job is to hold her accountable to the best version of herself," says the coach. "She knows that does not involve screaming at work."

We have observed that some leaders turn nasty to compensate for deficits that they perceive in themselves. A person who treats others arrogantly, for example, is likely to be insecure. "Arrogance is a way of distancing yourself from the emotional pain caused by who you *think* you are," says Gene Early. "Working with a coach helps orient you to the essence of who you *truly* are so you can release denial of that pain and be free from any insecurity." The positive results are internal peace, a deepened rapport with others, and improved communication.

At times, all a leader may need is to be reminded of another's humanity. One coach described a client named Anthony, an especially overbearing executive at an insurance giant. He had informed the coach early on how much smarter he was than his peers. When the coach visited him at his company, Anthony ignored his assistant, who was stationed just outside his office. "She's not very good," he told the coach. "She just sits there." The coach responded that the assistant sounded like an underutilized resource. She suggested that Anthony talk to the assistant about his role and explore ways that she could help him.

The next time the coach visited, the assistant had completely reorganized Anthony's office and was working on other projects for him. "He had made an assumption that she was lesser, and what he did was too complex for her to understand," says the coach. "It just took him talking to her to turn a bad relationship around."

Everyone should aspire to something in their leadership that is nobler than simply not being a jerk. Coaches love working with C-suite denizens because, if they are both good and good at their jobs, then they have the power to make a big positive difference. Carol Kauffman describes her responsibility coaching top executives as "caring for and confronting the powerful and galvanizing their goodness so they can become forces for good."

You will get more from coaching if you redirect your goals away from jerk-like self-aggrandizement and purely personal gain. One of the leading women's leadership coaches, Sally Helgesen routinely asks female leaders not what they intend to do or to be, but instead what they intend to contribute. Women, she says, are often more comfortable with the language of contribution than of achievement. It's a wonderful question for all leaders because it sets goals in the context of serving others and acting as part of a larger organism.

Then there are the hard cases. Meanness is bred in the bone. Although cartoon villainy in the C-suite is rare, a full-blown Captain Hook or Cruella de Vil can be found in some organizations. The causes behind their unpleasantness are varied. A traumatic childhood, a rotten marriage, even a lousy golf handicap. Addressing these evil seeds is the job of therapists, professional examiners of their client's personal life and how that intersects with their work life (if applicable). Coaches, on the other hand, are professional examiners of their client's work life, career, and influence on others in business. It just so happens that in most cases, the leader learns something about themselves that affects their personal life, too.

And sometimes coaches must fight fire with fire. Coaching is a process designed for grown-ups, calling for no sugarcoating or awarding of participation prizes. Marshall recalls dealing with the CEO of a big pharmaceutical firm, whom we'll call Bill. The problem with Bill, his board realized, lay in his extremely abrasive behavior that was prompting capable subordinates to skedaddle for the exits, their hair on fire. So, they called in the best to somehow inspire personal change in what was an otherwise competent CEO.

But Bill was having none of it. He had no need of any coach, and the board was peopled by fools. Marshall gently reminded him that while Bill's job held a lot of power, there were still other decision-makers who had more power than him, namely, board members with the ability to fire in a heartbeat.

Peter Drucker taught Marshall many great lessons, one being: "We are here on earth to make a positive difference, not to prove how 'smart' or 'right' we are." Another great lesson is: "Every decision in the world is made by the person who has the power to make the decision—make peace with that." A third lesson is: "When we need to influence the ultimate decision-maker to make a positive difference, that person is the customer and we are a salesperson. Customers never have to buy—salespeople have to sell."

Bill realized that the board and his key stakeholders were not "buying" what he was trying to sell.

"What should I do, Marshall?" Bill asked.

Marshall suggested that Bill ask all of his stakeholders, including the board, for confidential feedback, listen to the feedback, and demonstrate humility rather than arrogance.

Pick an important behavior to change, follow up, and get better!

Bill turned out to be a great example of a leader who changed in a very positive way.

THE IMPORTANCE OF SLOWING DOWN

Take a deep breath. And now take another one. Why? Because if you are a hard-charging leader, you are probably as swift as the wind. And that becomes a problem, both in normal business life and in a coaching engagement. It impedes rather than speeds progress.

We know that the kinds of people served by executive coaches typically are very smart and work through problems very quickly. They have wowed leaders above them, which is how they achieved their current stature. But it's a small step from impressive to intimidating.

Monica, a fast-rising leader at a logistics company, did not mean to deprive people of oxygen. But her brain worked so rapidly that she unintentionally smothered the participation of others. Early in meetings, Monica would come up with a solid idea incredibly quickly, and her colleagues felt at once it almost certainly would be the best produced. That false certainty stunted the contribution of alternative inputs, limiting the team's potential for innovation. "The stakeholder feedback was, 'I don't feel like I am being included in discussions,' and 'I want more input,'" her coach remembers them saying. The coach worked with Monica to refrain from speaking until those around her had had their say. He also urged her occasionally to defer to the opinion of someone else. "We wanted them to see they could pop in with an idea, and she would acknowledge and go along with it," says the coach.

Monica was empathetic and considerate of her colleagues' feelings. But, complicating matters, many super-smart leaders project their own characteristics onto others, a cognitive bias that Marshall calls the "Why Can't They Be Like Me?" fallacy. These leaders can't figure out why the rest of the world isn't functioning at the same elevated level as they are. If you've always been an uber-achiever, then your breakneck speed feels normal to you. You may lose sight of those left in your wake—or not give them a chance to show they can keep up.

Carol Kauffman calls this "Superman syndrome." "You shake someone's hand, and they walk away with crushed bones," she says. "You relate to people in a way that makes them feel overwhelmed, stupid, anxious, and devalued. They don't understand what you just said. And they don't have permission to say, 'I don't understand.' Has it ever occurred to you that you are scary? Why do you think people dive into their offices when you walk down the hall?"

By slowing down, you can soothe ruffled feathers. And pause to hear what your coach has to say. Examples abound about the perils of speeding. One coach described Kevin, a director of a medical-device manufacturer. His brilliance and productivity were propelling him ever higher in his organization. "But he is not bringing anybody along with him," says the coach. "He is so far ahead that he is leaving people out." Kevin talks fast, finds it impossible to slow down, and doesn't see why he should. Clearly, he believes it would be better if everyone else just kept up. "He can't hide his frustration with people," says his coach. "And they, in turn, don't want to work with him or for him."

Being intimidating compounds the shortage of feedback, a major problem for leaders and one that we mentioned at the outset when describing the plight of our poor gorilla CEO. The higher you rise, the less willing people are to tell you the truth.[9]

Although employees may tremble, the business world is still impressed by leaders who think and talk fast. But that can have a corrosive effect. Stephen, CEO of a luxury goods company, told his coach that after a board meeting, he felt like a large weight was lodged in his neck and chest. He and the coach diagnosed it as exhaustion. As they probed for a cause, Stephen explained that he felt pressured to answer questions "professionally." In his mind, that translated to "fast." The coach had already observed that. "Before I finished a sentence, he would have an answer," she says. Using a stopwatch, she began asking Stephen simple questions, not permitting him to respond until five seconds had elapsed. Then she raised it to ten.

More digging produced an origin story. Stephen had been a poor student as a child and started talking fast because he associated that behavior with intelligence. "He trained himself to do this," says the coach. "And it was killing him inside."

Even if you're not intimidating people with your speed, you may be confusing them. And because you are who you are, no one will tell you that. You can learn a lot by asking your coach to listen to you talk to your workforce. Coaches can put themselves in the shoes of a person in the organization and say, "If this isn't clear to me, then it might not be clear to your colleagues."

So, before your coach first darkens your doorway or lights up your screen, you should already have resolved to take your foot off the accelerator. You'll need to slow down before you can turn the ship around. As they say in the US Navy SEALs, slow is smooth, and smooth is fast. Putting it into a lower gear will benefit your workforce and enhance your coaching sessions. Though we know you can move fast, we recommend that you move fast on slowing down.

Coach Selection Prework

Your coaching journey starts even before you select a coach. In this section we clarified your expectations from the coaching process and provided suggestions to make your coach selection journey a successful one.

- **Do your homework.** You must exercise care in finding a coach. The three avenues to finding a coach are through a blind search, a personal referral, or via a coaching agency. Regardless of the method you use, we recommend speaking to a few different coaches so that you can make an informed decision. A good fit makes a big difference.
- **Know what's important to you.** Executive coaching is a wide and varied world. Countless types of coaching methodologies, specialties, styles, and formats exist. When meeting coaches, keep an open mind to hear why they employ certain methods but don't be afraid to express what's important for you in a coaching relationship.
- **We all are jerks at some point.** We all have flaws and room for growth. Leaders, while more scrutinized, often receive less feedback, which can lead to unnoticed negative perceptions. Coaching can help both in identifying the flaw and correcting it, holistically and in a way that resonates with others.
- **Understand your intentions.** Coaching is focused on your growth. But it's also important to remember that leadership involves others. You will get more from coaching if you expand your goals beyond purely personal gain and focus

on the contribution you can make to the world and those in your orbit. You can be a force for good.

- **Remind yourself of your coach's priorities.** In executive coaching, an expert coach applies motivation, psychology, discovery, and discipline to help you develop self-awareness and make progress toward your goals. The coach is hired to prepare you to fill both your own and your employer's needs. But they are always in your corner , regardless of whether you or your company are paying for your coaching.
- **Slow is smooth, and smooth is fast.** Leaders, particularly high-achievers, often operate at a rapid pace. In both leadership and coaching, speed often hinders progress. A lightning-fast leader might confuse others or leave them behind. In coaching, a leader will begin making shifts; one must slow down a fast moving vehicle in order to make a turn.

If you do the work of selecting the coach that is right for you, you may be surprised by how non-transactional the relationship with your coach will feel. Yes, they are being paid. But they take your wins and losses almost as personally as you do. They will genuinely care about you.

CHAPTER THREE

GETTING STARTED

POINT OF DEPARTURE

Okay, we've thrown a lot at you. How do you start? If you are a jerk and you need to get better, can you really do so? Yes, you can. Everything we are sharing is possible for you to achieve. But possible is not always easy. We are going to share a few things to remember, and then we'll tell you some tricks of the trade of the most powerful coaches. First and foremost, let's remember that coaching is a human endeavor. In fact, business is a human endeavor. Both require a robust give-and-take. So be prepared to spill the tea at your first meeting with a coach.

At that meeting, your coach will want to know as much as you are willing to share. Don't hold back. Even before the first face-to-face of your engagement, they may ask you to answer questions about how you work, your communication style, the challenges you face, the people you admire, and your proudest moments. Some coaches get creative with their questions.

Michelle Tillis Lederman, for example, asks her clients to share a favorite leadership quote and why it speaks to them. Such questions are meant to reveal insights about what drives you, your values, and your self-awareness.

During the launch meeting, your coach will probably ask you to relate your life story, asking you to pay special attention to defining moments, such as when your life changed or when you experienced a sudden insight or flash of clarity. Many coaches pay particular attention to "origin stories." As Gene Early says, "They explain a primary source of your compelling motivation that persists through time and across contexts of your life. Recognizing this story can put many life puzzle pieces together and make meaning for yourself and others about who you are and why you do what you do."

Those stories are powerful and likely will emerge again and again throughout the engagement. One coach was helping Nguyen, a hospital administrator who was agonizing over a decision to fire someone. She asked him if he recalled when he first decided to be a kind person. Nguyen replied with a specificity that surprised her: when he was four years old. He was living in a refugee camp at the time, he told the coach. An older girl was trying to take food from him, and his mother told him to defend himself. "His mother said, 'You need to punch her,'" says the coach. "'And if you don't punch her, then I will punch you.'" The child refused. His mother punched him in the face. From that story, the coach gained insight into Nguyen's strongly held values instilled by suffering, which informed her subsequent coaching.

Fully enabling this level of sharing can be challenging for many. The reason is straightforward: It is hard to be vulnerable. We are conditioned from a young age to avoid exposing ourselves to risk or rejection, and sharing personal information can do just that. For many, it takes a stated commitment to allow ourselves to be vulnerable; to feel fear and do it anyway, as the saying goes. And it is well worth the effort, as it frequently provides the unlock for you and your coach to do your best work together.

Your coach will also look for patterns in your stories and responses to questions, and even in your choice of words. How you talk about yourself reveals a great deal. Do you share a lot or very little? How do you describe your impact? Do you speak in terms of strategic goals or operational details? "We're looking at how you present yourself in the narrative, and can you go bigger?" says David Noble. "You need to mentally elevate yourself. You need to see the bigger context for what you have done."

Peter Bregman looks for disconnects—for example, the difference between how you spend your time and what you say actually matters to you, or between the position you hold and your career goals. Opportunities, he says, lie in the gaps. "Say you are the CEO of a family-owned conglomerate where you can't make your own decisions," says Peter. "You don't know why you're frustrated? I'll tell you why. It's because you aren't free to make your own decisions."

In these conversations, total candor is essential. Don't exaggerate your successes or downplay your failures. Don't claim nobler motivations than you have. And, whatever you do, don't try to impress your coach. They've seen it all. They operate in a no-bamboozle and judgment-free zone. "At the first meeting, when someone says they are self-aware more than once," recalls a coach with a smile, "then I know that they are not self-aware."

Your coach will also ask you about your goals and the obstacles in your way. Sally Helgesen asks leaders to create a buzzword-free intention statement that sets out their larger purpose in the world. "Often, people come to coaching because specific circumstances are causing them pain," she says. "An intention statement gets them in a reflective mood and helps them focus on the bigger picture. This helps them be more intentional about positioning themselves to achieve their ultimate goals."

Peter Bregman frames this early challenge as solving the right problem. As he explains, becoming a swift, sound decision-maker is a worthy goal—unless the urgent challenge is building out your team. "If we identify what we need to work on before we identify where we are headed, it's a shot in the dark whether we're working on the right stuff," says Peter. Coach Nilofer Merchant compares this to the navigational skill of orienteering. "To get to a new level of performance, people need to define where 'there' is and, equally, 'here,'" she says. "It's when we know the specifics of those two points of reference—for this person, at this point in time—that we can effectively chart a course of action that addresses the specific obstacles and terrain."

Almost immediately, you and your coach will identify one or two areas to target for improvement. Then you will create a development plan using a format likely specified by your coach. It might comprise some broad goals broken down into discrete actions further distilled into daily checklists. The aim is to start small, taking the first baby steps of a long journey. There is no use in embracing the entire itinerary all at once and certainly not at this first meeting. Coaching aims for results, not ambitions. Getting off to a modest start guarantees an initial success on which you can build over time with your coach. Some call this "turning the flywheel": finding that initial action or success that starts the momentum and leads to more.

Let's take an example of one such baby step. Assume your goal is "communicating with patience and respect." Your action items might include slowing your rate of speech and starting conversations with curiosity by asking a question. You should practice the new behaviors every day, perhaps enlisting a friend to remind you. "You want very specific, observable, measurable actions," says Michelle Tillis Lederman. "You want to be able to say, at the end of the day, 'Did I do this? How consistently did I do it?'"

As the engagement progresses, the agenda should be in your hands. Many coaches will start each meeting by asking what is top of mind, what challenges you face in the moment, or simply how they can be of service. "I have a client who starts out every meeting with, 'Unless you have something else on your agenda...,'" says one coach. "I say, 'No, the agenda is yours.' We rarely get back to what we were going to work on. And that's fine. Because she knows what she needs to talk about at that moment."

Also, don't think of your meetings as transactional. "You aren't going to walk away from each session with a new skill," says Beth Polish, "but your coach wants you to get something valuable from every hour you spend with her." Beth concludes all her sessions by asking, "Did you get what you needed today?"

STAKEHOLDER-CENTERED COACHING

Now comes the first bump. Very early on in the engagement, our coaches move from the one-on-one to the many-on-one, enlisting people beyond the leader in the coaching process. This method is called Stakeholder-Centered Coaching, which Marshall established with the goal of providing the executive a comprehensive, 360-degree review of their leadership—what the French call *un tour d'horizon*. Here's a high-level review of what you can expect from this common coaching process.

Your coach will ask you to identify your key stakeholders. These could be your manager, peers, colleagues, and direct reports. If you are the CEO, you might include board members. Perhaps a spouse or other family members belong on the list—after all, those external to your organization play a strong role in your behavior and patterns at work. Choose people you interact with in different ways and who likely will have disparate opinions of you.

Stakeholders are usually very willing to give feedback directly to a coach, even if they wouldn't share it with the leader, for two reasons. First, because they are *asked*. Most leaders do not take the time to earnestly ask people for their thoughts and feedback and provide a psychologically safe environment for them to share it. Secondly, because the coach serves as a buffer to make the feedback totally anonymous. Coaches collate feedback into themes and anonymize any quotes. Even if the leader thinks they know who said what, they should *never* retaliate. That will guarantee that feedback is never provided again. And honest feedback is at the core of a successful coaching engagement.

Coaching opinion varies widely on the number of stakeholders to recruit: from as few as five to as many as twenty-five or more.

We often recommend that leaders ask their manager, or if they are the CEO, the board to review the list and check that they have not left out anyone critical.

Your coach will interview those stakeholders and solicit confidential feedback regarding your habits and performance. The operative word is confidential. Once again, candor is the goal. The coach will probably ask some version of the following five questions about the client they're coaching:

- What are they doing well?
- What do they need to do better?
- What situations bring out the best in them?
- What situations bring out the worst in them?
- Any suggestions—either big picture or practical—that might help them be a better leader or have a better life? For example: They should examine how they treat women in the workplace. Or: They should put away their cell phone during face-to-face conversations.

Individual coaches may have their own variants of questions to pose. John Reed asks stakeholders to design the perfect day and the worst possible day for the leader in question. Jennifer Goldman-Wetzler wants to know how each stakeholder influences the client's leadership and what they could do more of to support them. The idea is to encourage collaboration and prevent someone with whom you have an issue from placing all the blame on you and making it your sole responsibility to improve things. Through this process, your coach collects valuable insight and begins the process of enlisting your stakeholders in your continued growth and success.

Your coach will compile all the feedback from the interviews into an anonymized, aggregated 360-degree report (commonly called a 360.) You may never have seen a report like this. It can be short, or it may be long. Regardless of the style or format, it may be sobering, perhaps surprising, but always illuminating—as long as you commit to and maintain an open and receptive mindset. You and your coach will go through it together, item by item.

Sanyin Siang emphasizes the need for self-awareness, which often requires external feedback (such feedback is provided in a 360). This feedback is vital to understanding how others perceive our actions and whether our intentions align with these interpretations. "We often don't see ourselves clearly, so we need data to do so," Sanyin notes. "Moreover, in order to grow, we need to understand our distinctive strengths as well as our opportunities for improvement."

For instance, Alice, a vice president at an energy company, had taken countless online personality assessments and received numerous electronic surveys about her from her peers and reports. But the 360 she received from her coach really took the cake. She described it as the single most valuable report she had ever read—like an operating manual for herself. Of course, there were surprises, but she could feel the candor and honesty through each word. She told us that she put the report on her kitchen refrigerator where she would see it every day.

You can tell your coach whether you agree or disagree with the individual comments, but we encourage you to really hear and accept the feedback. Your stakeholders want to help you. From the proffered suggestions, you will choose a few high-level pieces to focus on, in addition to the baby steps identified in the first meeting. Two examples: I want to be a better listener; I want to control my frustration.

Yes, you will meet with your coach to map out a plan to achieve those goals. It is not enough to simply make the change; you will also need to enroll your stakeholders and take them on the journey with you if you are to change their perceptions of you.

At some point, you will meet with each of your stakeholders and tell them about what behaviors or skills you are working on improving as a result of your learnings from the 360 assessment. Here is what we believe you should say to each of your stakeholders, irrespective of whether you agree with the feedback or not: "Thank you very much for taking the time to talk to my coach and share your feedback. Your feedback can help me develop and become a more effective leader. I'm grateful for your support in my growth." That's it. If we can commit to just saying thank you, it seals the experience and affirms goodwill. It also leaves the stakeholder more open to continuing dialogue in the future, if and when you need it.

One other thing to consider here, in addition to a thank you: If your intuition tells you that you need to apologize for your behavior because it's obvious that the person has been hurt by it, do so. Again, this is not the time for a story, but rather something specific and succinct, along the lines of: "I'm sorry I haven't always listened to you and the people around you. I see that now. And I'm working on steps to address it."

It is part of the Stakeholder-Centered Coaching process to have brief, occasional check-in meetings with your various stakeholders. These meetings generally need not be longer than five to ten minutes. The point is that you do them. If you do, you will collect valuable ongoing feedback. You will improve, and your stakeholders' perceptions of you will certainly change for the better. Marshall's research involving over 86,000 participants, chronicled in the article "Leadership is a Contact Sport"[10] and published by *Strategy+Business*, confirms it.

You will then ask the stakeholder for ideas about how you can improve in the future, with "future" being the imperative word. We want to leave the focus on the past behind as soon as possible. Two examples: "How can I do better for you?" and "Do you have any suggestions that might help me become a more attentive, open-minded listener?" Asking these questions can be difficult, and stakeholders can find it challenging to respond honestly—but by opening with a message of thanks and clear acceptance of the feedback, you've already made it easier for them to answer truthfully.

It's important to note the reality of power dynamics in the workplace and how they can directly impact your feedback. There is always potential for your direct reports to have apprehension about participating in the 360 assessment or other feedback-gathering processes—particularly if your organization does not typically foster a culture of open communication and proactive feedback. Your direct reports may not fully trust in the anonymity the coach is providing or be inclined to take the chance to discuss in person how you can improve.

In our experience, this type of apprehension rarely happens. Usually, participants are thrilled to contribute to a leader's growth and development. After all, your direct reports are likely the biggest beneficiaries of your improved leadership. And if you have a good coach, they will have set up the 360s in such a way that minimizes participant apprehension. However, as a leader, it is your responsibility to be keenly aware of how a stakeholder is sacrificing some level of security (even if the risk is very low) to participate and provide constructive feedback. Regardless of who the stakeholder is sitting across from you—but *especially* if it's a direct report—the following instruction is imperative.

Sit quietly and take notes while the stakeholder talks. Do not interrupt. This is not the time to comment or push back against their ideas, nor should you promise to implement them. Instead, simply say you intend to consider all the good ideas you are hearing and do what you can to improve. Again, you will say thank you. Feedback is a gift, and your ability to feel heartfelt gratitude will greatly enhance your potential to extract what you need from it. As with all priceless gifts, thank you is the best and only appropriate response.

We know it can be hard to overcome defensiveness, but we have also heard countless stories of the rewards that come as a result. Clara, a mid-level manager in consumer packaged goods, had developed a reputation for being somewhat defensive, often reacting to feedback from stakeholders with resistance. She began the coaching process and dutifully met with each of her stakeholders to hear their feedback and suggestions. In one such meeting with a direct report, Elise, she received what she perceived as unfair or unjustified criticism. However, she recalled her coach's steadfast advice to simply respond with "thank you" and withhold any defensive retorts.

Summoning every ounce of self-control, Clara managed to keep her thoughts to herself, allowing Elise to express her concerns without interruption. Elise, grateful for the opportunity to be heard without confrontation, felt a sense of relief and appreciation. In time, Clara began to see the value in Elise's perspective, and she found herself seeking her input on an increasing number of topics.

This newfound openness not only significantly enhanced their professional relationship but also fostered a spirit of collaboration that extended beyond the company. A year later, the two joined forces and embarked on a successful entrepreneurial venture together.

As you go through the process of meeting with your stakeholders for the first time post-360, feel free to debrief with your coach. Here is what this person said. Here is what I learned. Here are their suggestions. Here is what I am going to do about it. Together, you and your coach will devise your development plan and action items. You will start working on them.

Two months later, you will again sit down with those stakeholders to see how they think you're doing. Two months after that, you'll do it again. Two months later, again. Continue to share your reflections with your coach. You will see what is working and what still needs work. You will see the change in you and in the perceptions of your stakeholders.

At the end of six months, the coach will often ask your stakeholders to complete a survey that includes a qualitative assessment of your progress. The results may not thrill you—perception shift usually lags behavior change. But they may motivate you— you will certainly see progress. If your engagement lasts a year, the coach will conduct another survey at the end. Likely, that one will go much better. It takes about a year for new behaviors to put down roots and for the perception of others to make a major shift. Finally, you will create your own system to ensure that you continue to improve and don't backslide. Remember, you will not always have a coach-whisperer.

Throughout this process, you must practice humility and respect, both of which are critical to good leadership. You are telling your stakeholders: I know that I am a work in progress. You deserve the best. Help me be that for you.

And they will help you. This process can turn rivals into allies. Embracing it is a powerful display of humility and vulnerability—a display we can describe in one word: leadership.

HELL IS OTHERS, OR MAYBE IT'S YOU

The 360 report can be a bitter pill to swallow. In our experience, reaction to it ranges from acceptance to apoplexy. One client, his temples throbbing, demanded one of our coaches supply him with an exact accounting of who had said what. The client lamented that he had hired the wrong people; now it was his turn to fire these malcontents.

This was a rare instance of extreme backlash, and one that did not bode well for the future of that coaching engagement, not to mention the future success of that leader. More common is gentle pushback. And this does not occur solely with the initial 360; throughout the coaching process, critical feedback is often dismissed as arising from the flaws and grievances of others.

"L'enfer, c'est les autres." "Hell is others," in the famous words of philosopher Jean-Paul Sartre, himself no paragon of heavenly behavior. We have observed that human relationships are at the core of most prompts to engage the services of a coach. And we ask ourselves, isn't it amazing that most problems arise from the bad behaviors of those who work with our client? Uncanny, really.

Here is an example: A high-ranking aerospace executive, Lucas, constantly shifted blame, pointing fingers at others for any failures. Despite his CEO's insistence on getting a coach, Lucas resisted, citing countless excuses. Eventually, the CEO had had enough and let Lucas go. This wake-up call shook Lucas to his core. Reflecting on his mistakes, he realized the importance of taking responsibility. Now leading a successful organization, Lucas credits being fired as the catalyst that transformed him into a more accountable, effective leader.

We all have things we can work on—it's part of being human. But it doesn't make sense to complain about others while we wait for them to change. We can only control ourselves, and great leaders lead by example. So, if you want others to change, you go first.

We recommend introspection. Might the problem be you? Physician, heal thyself? We are not saying that you are the demon, and your workplace irritants the angels, but perhaps you should sit back, close your eyes, and think. You may realize that in each case there was one consistent common denominator: you.

Are your problems always someone else's fault? "My boss disrespects me." "My direct reports don't follow orders." "This other vice president keeps shooting down my ideas." In that case, you may feel you don't need to change anything but your job. The coach, who wants to help you change, can only do so much. And you may find that the old adage is true: No matter where you go, there you are. Take a moment to reflect, without judgment, if this is a pattern in your life. If so, that is likely a place to explore with your coach.

"If you find yourself saying to your coach, 'Here are all the things other people are doing wrong,' then it might be a rocky start," says Whitney Johnson. "That doesn't necessarily mean that things won't change. But that is an initial indicator that coaching might be a challenge for you."

For coaching to work, you must bring a more humane interpretation to your relationships. "It's very rare that you would find yourself in a situation where everyone around you is terrible," says Sally Helgesen. "So, you need to ask yourself, how am I playing into this dynamic?" The coach's job, in these situations, is to help ineffective or antagonistic relationships evolve, not listen to a weekly report of "You'll never believe what he did this time!"

Give introspection a try. Perhaps you are more responsible for workplace tensions than you realize. Say your boss consistently downplays your contributions. Have you had similar experiences with other people? Are you sure you understand the problem or the person's motives? Maybe they are acting for reasons you haven't considered. You might talk to others who have worked for or with them. Did the same things happen? How did they handle it?

Or toss the cards in the air by meeting hostility with generosity. Reframe the question from "How do I put up with these people?" to "How do I serve these people?" A little emotional creativity can go a long way.

Karen, a vice president at a consumer goods conglomerate, got off to a bad start when she was transferred from her company's headquarters to a branch in another country, where her new colleagues seemed to distrust her and froze her out. "We talked about how she could be useful to them," says her coach. "She started arranging visits to the branch from senior people at headquarters, where Karen had worked and knew a lot of people. That brought her new unit more visibility and opportunities," which was good for her colleagues. In turn, they began to accept her more, and Karen became more integrated into her new team over time.

We can't see our own faces, only a reflection. Similarly, we can't see our own behavior; we need reflections from other people. These reflections help us to see ourselves more clearly and understand the actions that can help us and those around us thrive. Self-awareness is only possible with the reflections of others.

So, if the 360 or subsequent feedback sessions put you in a defensive crouch, where you point your finger at hellish others, perhaps you should give yourself a time-out. Those others are the people you rely on and are charged with leading. Give them a break. Take the time to process what you have heard, extract the learning that will benefit you and your team, and leave the rest behind.

GOING BEHIND THE FACADE

It is time for a parable. One of the authors knows a young, well-off couple in Los Angeles. A baby on the way, they decided the time had come for a change of address. They went for a beautiful home in the hills: spacious, airy, and gleaming. It seemed to be a true "California Dream" home.

The move completed, they settled in. Within a few days, they noticed paint starting to chip off the living room wall. Huh? On inspection, they realized the paint was fresh, having been applied only in the last month or so. Worse yet, the paint was covering some nasty-looking wallpaper that had not been removed. The realtors had pulled a fast one. Instead of thoroughly fixing up the house for sale, they simply slapped paint on a problem to conceal it and to make everything look sparkly and new. And the problem was not trivial. On further inspection, the couple noticed the wallpaper was blackening, a telltale sign of mold. Tap a little farther in, and they saw that the mold was spreading to the sheetrock. The place was becoming a health hazard, no place for them to live, much less a newborn. Thus began a very expensive renovation, which required them to flee to a costly hotel for weeks while a contractor set about tearing down and building back up. It was as if they had pulled back the curtain on the Wizard of Oz.

Their tale of woe is instructive for our purposes. Coaching requires that a client change from within. The deep-tissue massage we mentioned earlier implies a profound process that reaches behind your public face. You really have to change, not just appear to have changed. Putting lipstick on a pig delays the inevitable comeuppance only for a time. If one of the goals gleaned from the 360 is, say, anger management, it does no one any good for you to put on a brave smile while seething with rage inside. Eventually the truth will come out. Your coach will tell you this again and again until you address it.

And sometimes such inner authenticity can lead to unusual outcomes. By opening yourself up to transformative behaviors, you also incur risk. In extreme instances, much of your life could be upended. Sometimes, people realize that they are at the wrong company or even pursuing the wrong career. Instead of climbing a ladder, they are walking a plank. One of our coaches remembers Yoni, a CFO at a scientific research company, struggling to collaborate with C-suite colleagues whose values were at odds with his. That disparity descended into animosity. The coach asked Yoni why he was still there. The idea that he could just leave "was so shocking to him," says the coach. But within the year, Yoni quit to become a master beer brewer—his life's dream.

Afterward, the company's president approached the coach and asked, "Are you coaching my people to leave me?"

"If they don't want to be here, do you want them to stay?" asked the coach. The coach didn't need to wait for an answer before following up his comment with, "You're welcome."

Thankfully, such life-altering epiphanies are not the norm. When you get behind your facade, you will probably not find mold—and if you do, your coach will help in your renovation. Together with your coach, you will begin to truly understand your inner workings and, if necessary, tinker with them. And if you exaggerate how closely you have examined yourself and how much effort you put in the process, we guarantee your coach will know. Eventually, that truth will be apparent to your peers and subordinates. The steps to becoming well and truly coached, from the inside out, is the subject of the next part of this book.

EXECUTIVE SUMMARY
Initial Steps to Change

The path to a successful coaching engagement starts small but can lead to transformative change. There are important steps to take to help improve your chances of coaching success.

- **Embrace openness.** Candor and openness to the process are essential for a leader to profit from a coaching engagement. Be prepared to share freely from the get-go.

- **Start small.** Almost immediately on first meeting, you and your coach will identify one or two attainable areas to target for improvement. The aim is to start small, taking the first baby steps in a long journey.
- **Gather and take action on feedback.** Expect the coach to solicit feedback from your stakeholders about you. Some coaches adopt a formal approach called Stakeholder-Centered Coaching or employ a 360 assessment. Together, you and your coach will review the feedback and may select some areas for development. But it is not enough to change one's behavior; you also need to involve your stakeholders if you are to change their perceptions.
- **You go first.** As humans, we all have areas to improve. Rather than complaining or waiting for others to change, we should focus on our own actions and lead by example. Seeking reflections from others aids self-awareness and provides insight into behaviors that can promote personal and collective growth.
- **Remember the importance of saying thank you.** Avoid defensiveness with your stakeholders. The phrase "thank you" is always the best response to the gift of feedback. This response fosters psychological safety and can even turn rivals into allies.
- **Take real steps toward change.** Faking a change of heart or a change in behavior will eventually fail. The coaching process thrives on honesty, integrity, and accountability.

These first steps will help you avoid the pitfalls that threaten the start of any coaching journey, including taking on too much, ensuring that you are set up for future success.

PART TWO

BECOMING COACHABLE

At this point, you've acquired a solid understanding of what coaching entails, who it benefits, and how to find the right coach for your needs. You've already embarked on the invaluable work of self-reflection and introspection, diving deep into your leadership patterns and clarifying your aspirations. Perhaps you've already identified some areas in which a coach can support your growth and help you attain your goals. Now, equipped with the knowledge of how to initiate a coaching relationship, we move on to the next crucial aspect: how to get the most from your coaching engagement.

By this, we mean you must now become well and truly coachable for the process to succeed. Rolling up your sleeves is the order of the day. While it's rare for a coach to conduct a scorched-earth policy and demand a complete overhaul, in many instances, they do solicit some major changes. It's up to you to be ready to tackle them head-on.

Sanyin Siang points out that to be coachable you must recognize your sense of agency. She says: "We are not defined by our past failures or past successes. In every moment we have a choice. We can choose to make a change or we can choose to stand still." There's no right answer here; we are free to make the choices we want, so long as we are willing to accept the outcomes of those decisions.

When we talk about becoming coachable, it's as simple as this: Open your eyes. No, really—open them. Openness is an integral part of the leader's coaching journey. It is the rack on which we hang our hat and the easel upon which we prop our canvas. And, it is the cornerstone of the framework we believe allows someone to become coachable.

The openness framework allows you to be ready for what the meatiest part of your coaching engagement has to offer—challenges, victories, and everything in between. It gives you the best shot at succeeding in this effort in which you're tasked to dive deep, stay centered, and move mountains. The four tenets within the openness framework require you to be open to **change, feedback, action, and accountability**.

As Marshall says: The process is simple, but that doesn't mean it's easy. The process of becoming coachable and, in turn, being coached, is a journey that demands steadfastness, resilience, and flexibility from you—and the reality is, the leader who is ready is the one who will embark on the challenge. Nothing about being a leader is easy, and, to most of us, it doesn't come naturally. Leadership asks difficult things of you every day: It asks you to set aside the person you may want to be because it's easier in a moment, for the person you *have* to be for the organization at large. So yes, leadership asks quite a bit of you. But if you wield the responsibility correctly, leadership returns infinitely more.

Commit the openness framework to memory, and you are ready to begin. Each of the tools in the openness framework requires a commitment to the process and the future. Our experience shows that these are the four keys that unlock monumental success and create coachable leaders. Not only that; they are also the traits of good leadership. So let's get started. Your future self awaits.

CHAPTER FOUR

OPEN TO CHANGE

CHANGE AS AN IMPERATIVE

How can you, as a leader, manage change if you're not willing to change yourself?

In *What Got You Here Won't Get You There*, Marshall explains how the same behaviors that powered an individual's professional ascent at some point start to stall it. Shifts in behaviors or actions are needed. Typically, this shift requires communication, humanity, compassion, and grace. You can cultivate additional virtues to foster change, and those related to temperament and behavior are often paramount.

Marshall's book focuses on individuals rising through organizations. Compounding the challenge, the organizations themselves are often undergoing rapid change: Perhaps they are growing fast, or becoming virtual, or they are under assault by disruptive innovation or navigating dozens of other dizzying transitions. "You can't scale an organization any faster than you can scale yourself," says Mark C. Thompson.

"With this accelerating pace of change, traditional playbooks for business and leadership are becoming less applicable. Leaders must create new playbooks in real-time, which presents a significant challenge, especially when it comes to mobilizing teams toward new directions," says Sanyin Siang.

As the world changes, so must the leader. Change is an important place to lead by example. Sanyin continues, "Leaders need to understand that the changes aren't just for everyone else; they must be prepared to alter their own ways too." Whether that means grappling with greater responsibilities or a mutating business environment, managing change is, arguably, the most fundamental skill of an executive. Coaching is among the most efficient, effective ways to master the ability to change. And for that, pardon the repetition, the client needs to be coachable and all-in on the project of personal renovation.

An important word on the motivation behind change. Leaders should not begin the coaching and change process just to get promoted. Great coaching clients change because they want more from their lives and expect more from themselves. There is a world of difference between Rising in an organization and Flourishing in life (and we'll get to both of those later). They overlap at points, but the life-changing achievements promoted by coaching have a more profound and lasting impact on organizations, personal well-being, and the world.

It is common for many of us to feel that we are not living as fully as we could be. That we are not as effective as we could be. That we are not contributing as much as we could be or making those around us as happy as we could be. But in many cases, we don't know precisely why we are falling short. Here, too, coaching helps delineate both the questions we are circling and their answers.

For example, Meredith, a highly accomplished senior partner at a major law firm, had worked tirelessly to achieve her professional goals. Despite her impressive career, she often felt overwhelmed, drained, and unfulfilled. Her demanding schedule left her little time for self-care or personal growth, and it began to take a toll on her mental and physical health.

After hearing about the transformative power of executive coaching, Meredith decided to give it a try. Her coach, a seasoned professional, focused not only on her career but also on her overall well-being. They explored topics such as work-life balance, self-awareness, and stress management.

As the weeks went by, Meredith noticed a shift in her mindset. She became more aware of her priorities and the importance of nurturing her well-being. She learned to set boundaries, delegate tasks, and make time for self-care activities that recharged her mind and body.

As a result, Meredith's performance at work reached new heights. Her relationships with colleagues and family improved, and she discovered a renewed sense of purpose and satisfaction in both her personal and professional life. Others took notice and sought out Meredith's guidance and mentoring, which became a deeply fulfilling part of her life. Not only did she continue to elevate her career, but she also achieved a profound, lasting happiness that resonated in every aspect of her life.

Without change, there is no growth. Without growth, there is no hope. In this, we echo the words of the Irish sage George Bernard Shaw: "Progress is impossible without change. And those who cannot change their minds, cannot change anything."

We all have deeply ingrained habits and patterns that can be difficult to become aware of, much less to change. Perhaps you think that you will never be better or happier because you will never be different from how you are now. "Growth is our default setting," says Whitney Johnson. "No one has ever met an 18-month-old who doesn't want to learn to walk. Sometimes people say, 'That's it. That's all I've got.' No, I don't believe that. Human growth is unbounded."

Change is hard. But it can also be exciting. It can be wonderful. Mark C. Thompson talks to leaders about the fear of change. At the end of those conversations, he asks them about their proudest moments. "I haven't had anyone who did not mention something that involved making a risky change and pulling it off," says Mark. "Whether I am asking someone to marry me, or going to college for the first time, or getting a big job. There was always change and risk involved."

Change is the imperative.

CHANGE AS AN ALLERGEN

We may have offended some of you earlier with our exposition of jerks. We will now double down: You may be allergic to change. Many of us are. Refusing the new is as old as the hills.

Potential coaching clients may act as if resistance to change is "baked in" to their personalities. People may believe their weaknesses and strengths are an unalterable part of who they are. They're as good as they'll get. And if they have risen professionally on those innate abilities, then they consider those sufficient. Some even recast their flaws as virtues. "Sure, I can be demanding and impatient, but, hey, my reports never miss a deadline."

Although change and growth are natural human states, the wellspring behind the instinct to resist can flood the path of our progress. There are three main culprits here: hubris, arrogance, and negativity. The highest hurdle arises from hubris. In other words, it's the know-it-all syndrome taken to the extreme. You believe you are perfect, infallible even. If you plan to hold on to that line of thinking, congratulations—you have the makings of a perfect cult leader.

Nathan, a charismatic CEO of a successful start-up, was one such leader. After a string of early successes, he believed his vision was flawless and grew increasingly convinced that he alone could lead his company to greatness. In his mind, he was a modern-day Moses, destined to guide his employees to the promised land of success. However, as the company expanded, his blind self-assurance stifled innovation and collaboration. Employees, intimidated by Nathan's unwavering conviction, hesitated to share ideas or challenge his decisions. Eventually, the company's progress stalled, and Nathan was forced to face the consequences of his unchecked ego.

In an article in *MIT Sloan Management Review,* Ben Laker, a professor of leadership at Henley Business School, explains that today's well-known CEOs are particularly susceptible to hubris because social media and a voracious business press have transformed them into brands and, in some cases, celebrities. And because hubris generally is associated with power, hubristic leaders often are in positions to do significant damage. Trusting their own track records and believing their own press, they unilaterally make decisions that hurt employees, shareholders, and customers.[11] Such leaders urgently need coaching. Hubris makes them unlikely to get it or be receptive to it.

Simply put, a coach cannot help perfect people improve. Coaching can only be utilized by a leader *wanting* to improve. If you are too proud to admit that you have a problem, then you won't try to conquer that nonexistent (in your mind) problem. Consequently, you will not get better. A good measure of humility is required for coaching to work.

Then there is the second culprit, which is the evil twin of hubris: arrogance. Hubris involves looking inward at your own glorious perfection; arrogance is looking outward at the manifest imperfection of the greater part of humanity that is oh so inferior to you.

Carla is a perfect illustration of this. She was the managing partner of a financially successful consulting firm, and she reveled in her own success. As she surveyed her industry peers, she saw only inferiority, her arrogance fueling disdain for those she deemed less accomplished. This contemptuous attitude permeated her company culture, and they openly mocked competitors, damaging how clients viewed the firm. Ultimately, this arrogance led to complacency and the company's downfall, as competitors outmaneuvered the firm and rose to prominence.

Obviously, coaching such arrogance is yet another exercise in futility, particularly when employing strategies that border on the touchy-feely. Arrogant leaders will reject these strategies out of hand, possibly laughing them off. But karma may get the last laugh; as we outlined in our sports metaphor near the outset, even the finest of natural athletes will be left in the dust if they are not coachable. The same fate eventually awaits the hubristic and the arrogant.

The third obstacle to embracing change stems from negativity, another habit of thought that bedevils many people. Leaders may say they want change and then shoot down every suggestion from their coach or stakeholders to bring about that change. It is akin to advocating for a balanced budget but voting no on every measure to cut spending or raise revenue.

One coach recalls Andrew, head of an investment bank, who rejected every suggestion she made. "Whatever I put in front of him, he would tell me why it wouldn't work and why he wasn't interested," she says. The coach concluded that the first behavior they needed to address was Andrew's instinct to start with "no." She persuaded him to notice every time he responded to someone with negativity and write down what he could have said instead. Andrew got better. "He may have adopted the new behavior only because it was a pain to keep writing things down," says the coach. "But it worked."

There are the few but formidable who stand on the commanding heights of authority. They are respected, perhaps feared. They have accomplished their decades-long ascent of the corporate mountain. Retirement looms in a few years, so why change anything at all? We understand that sentiment. They are at the "there" in Marshall's formulation of "what got you here won't get you there." But we posit one's potential for growth—whatever rung on the corporate ladder you may occupy—is never exhausted. At any age, it can be unleashed with beneficial outcomes for a person as an individual in a business, a community, and the world.

OF GROWTH MINDSETS AND
HEALTHY CONFIDENCE

In her book *Mindset: The New Psychology of Success*, Stanford psychologist Carol Dweck calls a view of oneself as immutable a "fixed mindset." People with fixed mindsets may avoid challenges, give up without a fight, and indulge in negative thinking. They would rather prove themselves right than learn. Those are hardly the behaviors of a successful leader.

Fixed mindsets tell people they can't change. Hubris says they don't have to. Hubris is an inflated sense of one's own abilities, often based on past success. A leader who informs their new coach that there is nothing they need to work on is displaying hubris.

In her book, Carol establishes that the opposite of a fixed mindset is a "growth mindset," which she defines as a state in which "people believe their most basic abilities and qualities can be developed and cultivated through dedication and hard work. Brains and talent are just the starting point." People with growth mindsets are in a constant state of becoming. They are ready to learn and expand. And they are inclined to bring others along on their journey. Naturally, they are excellent candidates for coaching.

This is not to say that the coached client should become a cowed acolyte sitting at the feet of a coach, pen and paper in hand, ready to transcribe words of wisdom later to be memorized. To the contrary, fostering a growth mindset requires a large heaping of confidence on oneself. And to be clear, hubris and confidence are not the same thing. While confidence, too, is a form of self-belief, it is not delusional self-belief. Confident people don't think they're infallible. They accept that they don't know everything. But they trust that they will overcome their shortcomings, conquer obstacles, and get the job done. Confident people are very coachable.

A note of warning: Doubting is healthy. Constantly doubting yourself, particularly if you make it a habit, can be debilitating. If you struggle with imposter syndrome, we recommend that you continuously choose to suspend your self-doubt when you feel it rise up. According to organizational psychologist and bestselling author Adam Grant: "Impostor syndrome isn't a disease...it usually means you're facing a new challenge and you're going to learn. Feeling uncertainty is a precursor to growth." Courageously choose to believe in yourself or, at the least, in the coaching process. You're worth it, and you'll get there.

Confident people tend to succeed, in part, because their belief is contagious. The brains of others respond differently to confident people than to people who lack confidence, according to researchers at the University of Sussex.[12] A confident person's opinion commands greater influence. People experience increased satisfaction when their own opinions align with those of confident people.

If you've risen to leadership or assumed it by starting something yourself, then you almost certainly are confident. You can imagine yourself at the finish line. But unlike hubristic leaders, you don't believe success is inevitable and every step you will take is correct. You know there will be spots along the racetrack where you will stumble, speed up too much, or slow down to look over your shoulder. If you improve your performance at those moments, you will not only win the race—you will win it in the best possible way.

NOT ALL CHANGE IS GOOD

Time now to curb our enthusiasm somewhat. We are not advocates of rashly storming the barricades to change, leaving the devil to take the hindmost. Goodness, no—certainly not rashness and especially not leaving others behind. Coaching does not embrace absolutes. It is imperative that you carefully examine any proposed change and weigh its possible benefits and downsides. The change in question may or may not fit with who you are and what you believe is right as a leader. Certainly, in the interest of self-awareness, you will want to consider what, if any, behavioral tic lies behind your decision to either participate or sit this one out. In other words, we recognize that change is not a universal solution, especially if it is change for change's sake.

We are all only too familiar with the deleterious effects of some change. Take an old Victorian building downtown that is inexplicably torn down overnight, only to be replaced with a gimcrack eyesore incorporating shoddy building materials and devoid of grace. Indeed, not all change is good. In her astute 1970 track "Big Yellow Taxi," Joni Mitchell sang, "They paved paradise, put up a parking lot." So, exercising a little caution before embracing change may be a good idea.

But embracing thought-out, vetted change is a must. Ever since the end of the sixth century BCE, when the Greek philosopher Heraclitus opined that change was the only constant in life, most of humanity has recognized that things never stay the same. Who, for example, had an email address thirty years ago, much less a social media presence? The trick is to go with the flow, but on your own terms. Rick Newman, a business journalist, put it well: "Change is not always a good thing. It may force us out of tired habits and impose better ones upon us, but it can also be stressful, costly, and even destructive. What's important about change is how we anticipate and react to it. Change can teach us to adapt and help us develop resilience, but only if we understand our own capacity for growth and learning. When change makes us better, it's because we have learned how to turn a challenging situation to our own advantage, not merely because change happens."[13]

Change is inexorably coming at you, whether you like it or not. We believe that it is up to each leader to decide if they should duck it or stand tall and be buffeted by it. In the end, it is a question of making the best possible judgment call in the moment.

THE DESTINATION IS UNKNOWN

Let's posit that you are open to change. You have a growth mindset and healthy confidence. You want to work with a coach to develop your abilities and identify what you don't see about yourself.

Before you pursue change, you must understand what you are changing from. Becoming the best leader that you can be requires thinking hard about who you are as a person, right now. Before you head into the unknown, you should explore the known.

"Coaching takes you from here to there," says Dean Miles. "We spend a lot of time thinking how great it will be when we get there. We don't spend nearly as much time on 'Where is here?'"

The strongest indicator of being open to change is not just willingness to become more self-aware but actual hunger for it. Dean describes the attitude that makes his coach's heart sing:

"I want to know everything there is to know. I want to use a microscope. I want to use a telescope. I want to see the smallest things and the things that are furthest away."

People with that attitude make wonderful coaching subjects. One business owner reached out to Derek, a sales leader, about his tendency to get into strained or contentious situations. He had recently been fired by a client and did not know why. Derek wanted the coach to help him figure it out. "You might say, 'Gosh, what a doofus. He doesn't know what he is doing wrong,'" says the coach. "But I liked the fact that he was open-minded. He was curious. He was able to say, 'The problem is me. Not them.' To me, that is very winning."

A coach may ask that you dig deep for the origins of your behavior patterns. Gene Early describes one process that is a test for openness. He asks, "Are you willing and able to access a reference experience?" Once the leader has identified that pivotal memory, the coach will work with them to trace patterns of decision-making and behavior that shaped their life, for good or for ill. Those patterns may impose "limiting views" on what the leader sees as possible or desirable.

In other words, the answers lie inside you. "The coach's job is to unlock that embodied knowledge, so you have access to all those resources," says Gene. Your coach doesn't presuppose an ability to instill something in you. The wellspring of all transformation lies not out there, but inside.

Examining who you are and have been will help you fix on the right goals: ones that are both realistic and likely to lead to personal satisfaction and professional growth. Despite our previous note that it is imperative to look toward the future whenever possible, this type of inward exploration is a moment in the coaching cycle during which it may be helpful to spend some time examining the past.

If you are frustrated, depressed, or burned out from the grind, remember that may be because you are not using the abilities that make you great. "Remember the advice, if you lose something, go back to the last place you recall seeing it," says Dean Miles. "Similarly, go back to that last time and place when you were at your best."

From the inner journey begins the outer one. Once you have established where you are, you'll have the desire to establish where you *want* to be, where you hope to end up. This desire is an understandable yet futile one.

There are no two ways about it: Coaching involves a journey into the unknown. With the help of your coach, you will discover new areas of interest and potential growth as you progress. Situations and people you thought you understood will reveal aspects of themselves that will surprise you. You may begin to question assumptions that have driven decisions you have made about your career thus far.

Whitney Johnson describes this journey as a kind of personal disruption. "You step back from who you are in order to slingshot into who you want to be," she says.

You won't put everything on the line at first, of course. As we explained earlier, when you start working with a coach, you will benefit by choosing one or two problems to address. "Specific objectives make coaching more successful," says Sally Helgesen. "And as you work on them, then the other areas you can work on open up."

As you advance from known problems to unknown opportunities, the need grows for concentration. Setting off to a familiar destination, you switch on your car's navigation system and mentally check out. But if your destination is not clear, you must direct your full attention to the road ahead and the surrounding landscape.

To realize the full benefit of coaching, says Dean Miles, you must show up ready to examine every aspect of yourself: mental, physical, spiritual, emotional, intellectual, professional, and familial. "We're not used to doing that. We are used to hiding and segmenting and protecting," says Dean. "To partner with your coach, you must bring all of you. And you must say, 'Let's be curious. Let's see what we can find.'"

It takes courage to do that. If you start to lose your nerve, a coach can help strengthen your resolve. Thomas, a banking CEO looking to change jobs, said he was wide open to anything in his next career. Thomas told his coach he wanted an adventure. The coach challenged him to make a list of thirty people anywhere in the world to whom he could reach out and request a chat about potential new directions.

For months and months, Thomas failed to produce the list. Finally, the coach told him to come up with just six names. "He was so excited when he delivered them to me," says the coach. "I said, 'These are six middle-aged White bankers who live in London. I am disappointed in you. You have got more imagination than that. Go do something else.'" Chastened, Thomas placed a couple of calls. He ended up at the helm of a major arts organization. "It was so cool," says the coach.

Trading the known for the unknown can feel risky for other reasons. You may have to sacrifice behaviors you think define you and open yourself to reconsidering relationships you thought were settled. Sometimes, the thing you must cast away is a role that has become central to your identity. It helps to remember that every time you vacate a spot, you create opportunities for people behind you. Still, if you love what you do, it is hard to let go. One renewable energy CEO, Theo, a thought leader in his industry, reveled in the attention he got from speaking at public events and doing interviews on television and in the press. "When these requests came in, he would go, 'Yes! Yes! Yes!'" says his coach. "He loved doing it. It was part of his identity as an expert."

Asked by the coach at the beginning of the engagement to describe his values and leadership style, Theo had said he wanted to enable others to rise. "Well, when he held that mic, someone else was not rising," says the coach. He guided him toward developing other people on his team to take over some of the public appearances. "That is what leaders do," says the coach. "And, honestly, there were more important things he could have been focused on."

Maybe you're enticed by the idea of discovering unexpected aspects of yourself. If all goes well, becoming coachable may make you a better human. Not only a success in business, but a success in life. You extend what you have learned in a coaching environment to the world at large—your family, your community, the planet. Or maybe not. You will know when you reach your unknown destination. And then go on to another one.

A MOMENT WITH MARSHALL:
OPEN TO CHANGE

The board of a Fortune 500 company hired me to work with the company's CEO. Apparently, the board had given the CEO guidance on how they wanted him to run the company and asked that he pay attention to their requests. When I met Calvin, he had all the swagger executives in high positions often have. A large Manhattan office with amazing views. A team of people made sure that he operated at peak efficiency. Unsurprisingly, his team listened to his commands and agreed with everything he said. Calvin was on top of the world.

During our first meeting, Calvin indicated to me that he was not open to change. He told me that, as the CEO of a big Fortune 500 company, he was hired to do what he thought was right for the organization. He espoused that all of his reports agreed he was doing an excellent job, that the company was growing the way he had predicted, and that the board should just let him do his job and stay out of his business.

"Calvin," I said, "you are right. You are the CEO of a Fortune 500 company, and that company is growing under your leadership. And all of the people who report to you tell you that you are doing a fine job, even an excellent job. And I also imagine that you are very well paid for this work, and I can see that you have a very nice office with excellent views. But you see, Calvin, the board has hired me to coach you because you are not doing the job they want you to do. You are not considering their requests. They feel your current behavior is not in the best long-term interests of the company."

Calvin replied, "Marshall, you should tell the board that they should mind their own business, and I will mind this business."

I saw this as an ideal coaching moment. "Calvin, you have a big and powerful job. But you see, those on the board have a more powerful job. While the board members do not own the company, they are the elected representatives of the ownership of the company. In other words, they do not report to you. You report to them. To put it plainly, CEO = good. Board = better. And they have hired me to work with you to accomplish the goals they have set, not the ones you have set. If you want, I can go back to them and let them know that you are unwilling to change, in which case I can tell you without a doubt they will fire you and find someone else who will do the job. Or we can work together—and you can work with them—to jointly determine what is best for the long-term interest of the company."

I could see the color go out of Calvin's face as he suddenly realized he was not as in control of his own standing as he had thought. At that moment, Calvin made a choice to become open to change—and in the long run, it served him very well. Calvin ended up developing a great relationship with the board and had a very successful twelve-year run as CEO.

Calvin was never a bad human being. He just let his job title go to his head.

EXECUTIVE SUMMARY
Embracing Change

Without change, there is no growth. Without growth, there is no hope. In the words of George Bernard Shaw: "Progress is impossible without change, and those who cannot change their minds cannot change anything."

- **Resist resistance.** Resistance to change may arise from hubris, arrogance, or negativity; all are tendencies you need to resist. Remember that change and growth are natural human states. Embrace them.

- **Adopt a growth mindset.** For adopting and adapting to change, it is useful for leaders to cultivate a growth mindset, whereby they believe their most basic abilities and qualities can be developed and cultivated through dedication and hard work. Brains and talent are just the starting point.
- **Find a healthy doubting balance.** Doubting is healthy. Doubting yourself too frequently can be debilitating. Find a balance between the two and pursue healthy confidence.
- **Change with a purpose.** Change for change's sake is inadvisable. Before embarking on a new course, carefully weigh the benefits and the possible downsides of a decision.
- **Know that it's never too late.** Regardless of your position or age, the capacity for growth and change is never depleted. This potential can be unlocked at any stage, bringing benefits to individuals within their professional roles, communities, and the wider world.

A coaching engagement will lead you into unknown territory. Be prepared to be pleasantly surprised, all the more so as the change you now envisage originated from within yourself.

CHAPTER FIVE

OPEN TO FEEDBACK

A BRIEF HISTORY OF LEADERSHIP

Given leadership's outsized impact across societies, researchers have long studied its nature over the years, including drawing important lessons from its evolution.[14] Imagine stepping into a time machine and heading back to the nineteenth century. The general consensus at that time, largely influenced by the Scottish philosopher Thomas Carlyle, was that leaders were born, not made. They were the superheroes of their time, blessed with a whole host of heroic traits like courage, charisma, intelligence, and a never-say-die spirit. In short, leadership was in their DNA.

But fast forward to the mid-twentieth century, and you'll see that leadership scholars have flipped the script. Kurt Lewin, considered the founder of social psychology, proposed that leadership styles could be classified into three main types: autocratic, democratic, and laissez-faire.[15] This behavioral approach was groundbreaking because it suggested that anyone could potentially become a leader, depending on their actions and behavior. The spotlight moved away from the inborn traits of leaders to the choices they made—in other words, their behaviors. It was a revolutionary idea—leadership could be learned. And if it could be learned, it could be taught. This shift paved the way for leadership training, executive education, and an emphasis on personal growth, including coaching.

And as we journeyed further in time, the notion of leadership started to become more democratic and inclusive. Bosses who ruled like emperors became less popular, and executives started to collaborate more. What's interesting is that as leadership roles changed, so did our expectations of leaders. About a decade ago, John Gerzema and Michael D'Antonio ran a major survey. They asked 64,000 people across thirteen countries about the qualities they most valued in leaders. The top picks? Inclusiveness, humility, and vulnerability.[16] These traits make leaders more open to listening to others and more caring about their thoughts and feelings.

Now, some might see this as moving the goalposts, but really, leadership is always changing. It's like trying to catch a wave—you've got to be responsive to the times, the mood of the moment, and the needs of your community or organization. Especially in today's world, where many organizations have a large influence, it's crucial for leaders at every level to be open to feedback. It's not just about being in charge; it's about being open to learning and growing, too.

ON BLIND SPOTS

Even if your Napoleonic dreams have been dashed and you are now ready to receive feedback, a fear can surface about what you will hear and how challenging the remedy will be. Perhaps you are aware that you don't always communicate clearly. Or you wonder whether you have rubbed some people the wrong way. So, you worry that when you open the gates of the 360, those flaws will come charging out and flatten you.

In the thick of that stampede will be flaws whose existence you did not suspect. These unpleasant surprises are called blind spots. It's a subject coaches talk about a lot. Blind spots can kneecap you if they cause you to miss crucial goings on in your immediate environment. In recent years, many leaders have been forced to acknowledge blind spots in the form of unconscious biases related to race and gender.

The feedback segment of Stakeholder-Centered Coaching pointedly targets blind spots about your performance as a leader. It occurs at the beginning of your coaching engagement and guides your initial decisions about where to focus.

For example, James, a senior leader at a leading hospitality company, had earned his position through years of hard work and dedication. He prided himself on his extensive knowledge of the company's processes and his keen eye for detail. Believing he was being helpful, James closely monitored every aspect of his team's work. Unbeknownst to him, however, he was actually micromanaging them, demoralizing their spirits.

This initial feedback identified a key blind spot for James, and he began to address it with the help of his coach. But if you are being coached, you should expect to continue the solicitation of feedback throughout the engagement—and should continue to seek such feedback well beyond the engagement when your coach is but a memory.

Correcting your assumptions and adjusting your behaviors may take time. But simply recognizing blind spots and identifying them as problems can launch you on a course to betterment. There's a saying among coaches: "Awareness activates agency." If you receive feedback, and your perspective shifts in a way that allows you to see a new path forward, act upon it. Do something. Inspire change in yourself, and your peers, reports, and organization will thank you.

Eliminating some blind spots can have an almost immediate, measurable effect on your leadership performance. Meena, an IT leader, assumed her team preferred her stoic, professional demeanor, so she rarely discussed her personal life. She cared deeply for her team to the point of being protective, and she tried to shield them from negative feedback. To her astonishment, the team desired openness in both areas. Overcoming this blind spot, Meena embraced her natural, transparent persona, sharing personal stories and constructive criticism. As a result, contrary to her expectations, she found that her team trusted and respected her more, not less. It is worth understanding how blind spots arise. You can even begin hunting for them before your coach solicits the first round of feedback.

Some blind spots are assumptions you make based on your own experiences or beliefs—as opposed to facts—that lead to poor decision-making. Imagine you have just left a company culture that valued candor. Everyone expresses their opinion. Your new company is more authoritarian. Dissent is frowned on and may even be punished. You send out a memo announcing important changes. When no one pushes back, you might mistake the silence for a universal acceptance rather than a reluctance to speak up.

Alternatively, the origins of a blind spot "may date back to how you were brought up," says John Reed. "This is how we did things in my family. As a child I was taught…" If your father ruled the family with an iron fist, for example, then you may not recognize that your own leadership style is distressingly authoritarian.

Perhaps most common are blind spots that result from insecurity. Victor, an executive at a toy manufacturer, wanted so badly to be liked by others that he subconsciously viewed every interaction as a pass/fail test wherein he would feel huge amounts of guilt if he didn't show up perfectly or if a joke didn't land well. This eventually caused Victor to avoid social interaction and become reclusive even as his team and family grew and needed him more. Insecurities make the prospect of owning up to shortcomings so painful that you refuse to acknowledge them out of a sense of self-preservation. "People with healthy egos have no problem confronting and learning things because it doesn't destroy them," says John.

Whatever their cause, blind spots can make leaders hard to work for or with. Conflict avoidance, anger, lack of follow-through on commitments, disrespect for others' ideas, discounting the importance of people's time, indecision, failure to communicate goals…the list of leadership glitches is a long and winding road. Exhibiting any of these traits does not make you a jerk, it makes you human. And establishing a culture of soliciting, accepting, and acting on constructive feedback is the key to combating individual blind spots.

As we discussed in Chapter Three, arguably the most common blind spot for senior leaders stems from a failure to set ego aside to fully consider valuable insights, innovations, and ideas brought to the table by others. Another such phenomenon: Some leaders are so passionate about their work that they misjudge employee commitment and enthusiasm. That blind spot is especially common among founder-CEOs and entrepreneurs, who love working until the wee hours and cannot understand why the office empties out at the end of the day. Alisa Cohn, one of the top start-up coaches and author of *From Start-Up to Grown-Up* says, "They may not realize other people are not as self-motivated as they are or don't care about the company as much as they do."

Another common blind spot involves intention versus impact. Say the CMO wants to emphasize his company's family-friendly culture. He publicly acclaims a senior manager for putting together some plans and schedules before going out on maternity leave. But in doing so, he ignores the rest of the manager's team who worked fifty-hour weeks for three months while their boss was away—ultimately demoralizing them. "The leader wants to believe he is justified by his intention," says David Noble. "He does not want to take responsibility for how that decision or action actually affected people."

Intent versus impact also engenders some of the racist and sexist incidents bedeviling companies. Tales of insensitivity and problematic behaviors abound in which, for example, a White person asks a person of color where they are from.

Another example: A coach was brought in when Nabil, a high-level medical practitioner, got called into HR for making inappropriate statements. The physician had advised a nurse he encountered in a hospital hallway that she should lose weight or go up a size in scrubs because the ones she was wearing were too small. "He thought he was doing her a favor," says the coach. "He was baffled about why she was upset." Coaching a leader through similar specific blind spots by providing targeted and constructive feedback only enhances the more general training they may receive from a diversity education program. Even if the leader is not enrolled in such a program, the feedback a coach provides—as long as it's salient, candid, and action-oriented—is often enough to spur concrete change with respect to the topics at hand. As long as, to the point of the last chapter, the leader is receptive to that change.

Sometimes, leaders may be blind to their own motivations. Fred, a CEO of a construction conglomerate, refused to act despite having received copious feedback that a member of his team was toxic for the work culture. "The CEO said the team member was important because he was implementing a certain system," says Fred's coach. But over time, the coach realized that the team member's job was protected because he served a different, more insidious function: Fred's scapegoat. "This person was the CEO's excuse when things weren't working," says the coach. "Fred was not emotionally aware that he was doing that."

On a more superficial level, blind spots can be patterns of speech or behaviors that you aren't aware of that irritate or insult other people. One coach recalls an executive whose facial expressions and eye-rolling projected his emotions with disturbing transparency. Every time the leader heard something he considered stupid or a question whose answer he deemed obvious, "he would give a look of, 'This is ridiculous. Why am I listening to this idiot?'" says his coach. The executive was in line to become CEO, a role that would include television appearances and making reports to Wall Street analysts. "He had to learn that part of the job is acting," says the coach.

Remediating behavior is never easy. But if you don't know that something you do—or don't do—is hurting other people or your own performance, then simply making that realization may push you far down the road to fixing it. And fixing it may spark incredible returns on team collaboration and, ultimately, innovation.

One fashion executive, a high performer named Susan, had created an emotional wasteland by ignoring feelings as she rushed to get things done. "I was really direct with her that this was a big problem," says Susan's coach. "She was completely surprised. She simply had no idea. As soon as she became aware of it, she set out to change things."

Feedback on blind spots may come out of the blue. We say that you should be ready for them. Instead of thinking of input as an incoming artillery shell, why not treat it as a gift that, if received properly, has the possibility to transform you, your team, and the organization at large?

HOW TO RECEIVE FEEDBACK

The practice of accepting and acting on feedback is at the heart of both Stakeholder-Centered Coaching and Marshall's overall coaching philosophy. It requires you to have the discipline to thank people for their input without judging or critiquing it.

It is not enough to feel open to feedback. You must also convince those providing feedback that you are open to it. That gives them a stake in your development and should encourage their participation in the coaching process and what comes after it. It also should keep the feedback faucet flowing. It is important to reward people for being critical of you. When you start arguing with the input, you stop getting the input. And without input, you can't grow and evolve into the leader your organization needs you to be.

There are nuances to how you accept feedback. The goal is for the leader and stakeholder to occupy a judgment-free zone. Pretend you've told your stakeholder that you want to be a better listener and ask for help. The stakeholder gives you three suggestions. You react to the first suggestion: "That's a great idea!" To the second suggestion: "That's interesting." To the third suggestion: no response. What you've done is grade those three ideas: A. C. F. But you are supposed to be equally, uncritically open to all feedback. So, do not grade it. Let it percolate, and thank the stakeholder for their suggestions. You never know what piece of feedback you might find resonating down the road.

Do not promise to do everything everyone suggests. Tell your stakeholders that you promise to listen to all the ideas and do the best you can. You won't disappoint them. Some people may think that you are not going to do anything, that you are not going to change. Some may even think it a waste of breath to voice feedback. It's up to you to prove them wrong.

The Stakeholder-Centered approach is a structured and controlled method of soliciting feedback. But there are others. Sally Helgesen uses a technique she calls "informal enlistment." Let's say you want to improve your presentation skills. On your way to a meeting, stop a colleague and tell her what you are trying to do. "You might say, 'I often seem to go into too much detail or offer too much background and end up losing my audience,'" says Sally. "'By contrast, I have noticed that you tend to be very concise. Would you watch me in this meeting and give me your feedback?'"

Sally also does formal 360s. But informal enlistment is lower stakes than questioning someone who works for you about how you can be a better boss, which asks that person to take a political risk. Because informal enlistment also encourages conversation, it can help leaders build and leverage useful relationships.

You may prepare yourself for the acceptance of feedback by thinking outside the professional frame altogether. Everyone has welcomed feedback at one time or another, at least in their private lives. Gene Early says, "Think about a person in your life you have listened to. Consider what enabled you to be open to that input—in all likelihood, you could see the truth in their feedback and felt safe with the person giving it. It's this type of environment that is key to all coaching relationships—in the executive setting and beyond."

When your spouse reminds you to watch your tone around the kids, they are, in fact, coaching you and providing feedback. Take a moment to reflect on how that feedback could apply to the workplace version of you. Such interactions occur at every turn in life, and you do not reject them out of hand. The same should hold true for a professional coaching engagement.

It can be good for your professional life to consider times you've been open to feedback in your personal life. And it can be productive to actively engage loved ones in the quest for feedback that you pursue at work. For most people, the same things we do wrong at work we do wrong at home. If you don't listen at work, then you probably don't listen at home, either.

If you don't give recognition at work, then you probably don't give recognition at home. In short, we take ourselves wherever we go. When accepting feedback, accept it holistically and unabashedly—and examine all areas of your life that feedback could potentially apply.

Coaches often will give leaders the option of including a family member or friend in the feedback portion of their coaching. Coaching addresses the whole person. Consequently, incorporating the input of family may improve your relationship with your spouse, siblings, kids, and parents. And, of course, your family knows you better than anyone. The most reliable insights you and your coach receive may well come from the people you live with.

Another advantage: If you hear the same feedback from both work and nonwork stakeholders, then you are less likely to blame office politics for any criticisms. Maybe you think, "My colleagues say I am a bad listener because they are jealous of me." Well, is your spouse jealous of you? Your kids? If they say the same thing, it may encourage you to view that feedback as truth.

Marshall offers this reframe on feedback: Instead of viewing feedback as uncomfortable, make it a game. Try to see how much feedback you can solicit in a given time frame. Of course, our refrain applies here: Offer no judgment, just say "thank you" each time. At worst, you will gain at least a few good pieces of perspective or advice. At best, you'll find intriguing nuggets of insight into yourself you may not have received otherwise. Don't be surprised if you join the ranks of others who call this exercise fun.

Marshall also likes to do the following exercise when giving a public address. He'll ask everyone in the audience to take out their mobile phones and text their loved one the question "What can I do to be a better partner in our relationship?"

Some of the answers verge on the hilarious. "Are you sick?" "Are you drunk?" "Who have you been sleeping with?" "Who was this message intended for?" Twice, though, the exercise saved a marriage. In one instance, an audience member asked his wife how he could be a better husband. And the wife replied, "We have to talk." This can be a dreaded phrase. Or, if you switch your perspective, it's a phrase that holds a world of possibility for improvement.

NOT ALL FEEDBACK IS GOOD

Time to hedge our bets once again. As with change, feedback can be hurtful, particularly if it's malicious in nature or verges on thoughtless input. Also as with change, you must separate the wheat from the chaff. Sometimes that can be difficult, and sometimes it is as plain as the nose on your face.

With that in mind, we have cooked up a beginner's cheat sheet that highlights examples of less-than-optimal input:

1. You are like a dog with a bone.
2. You are too outspoken.
3. You are too ambitious.
4. You should not ask hard, uncomfortable questions.
5. You are angry.
6. You care too much.
7. You are being too critical.

We cannot go forward here without speaking specifically about women, many of whom suffer the slings and arrows of outrageous feedback. We have already touched on, gently, the lasting influence of sexism. Thousands of years of patriarchy cannot be wished away; its legacy remains with us, always ready to rear its head, even in this beginning of the third millennium of the Common Era. A woman executive who speaks up and speaks her mind is often relegated, explicitly or in an unspoken manner, to the category of the brassy, sassy, pushy, and ultimately strident female. The resulting feedback is toxic and useless.

In her highly entertaining podcast, "We Can Do Hard Things," activist Glennon Doyle devoted an entire hour-long segment to women facing an onslaught of uninvited feedback.[17] Glennon, whose memorable motto is "Be messy and complicated and afraid and show up anyway," compares feedback to an actual physical mailbox filled with unsolicited mail. She counsels women to chuck the great majority of it into the recycling bin, because input provided to women is often overwhelmingly gendered and plain unproductive. Examples include feedback related to looks (think: criticism of female politicians), relationships ("When does she see her kids?"), and perceived personality ("She's so bossy"). Women may be characterized behind their backs as too ambitious and money-oriented, when in reality, they have the same goals as their male counterparts. And the feedback may contain snark—something Glennon says is cause for immediate jettisoning.

When what a woman contributes is looked at on its own terms, she says, then that is time to assess the criticism. Glennon claims that more than 90 percent of feedback directed at women amounts to nothing more than junk mail. While we have no way of verifying that number, it serves as a cautionary tale requiring what she calls "survival strategies" to withstand harmful, empty feedback. Without embracing Glennon's maximalist view of rotten feedback, we can only counsel both women and men to look carefully at the source, the content, and the tone of the input before deciding whether to take it to heart.

THE NOBILITY OF HUMILITY

The H-word. Humility. We are not advocating for church-mouse timidity here, only for an awareness of one's fallibility. We know that to be coached, you must at least tolerate input. But how much more powerful would it be if you had the humility to fully embrace it?

As we explained earlier, Carol Dweck of Stanford argues that people with a growth mindset recognize they can improve. People with intellectual humility recognize something just as important: that they may be wrong. The intellectually humble are willing to question their own beliefs, the evidence on which those beliefs are based, and the blind spots that may distort them.

Intellectual humility, says Mark Leary, a professor emeritus of psychology and neuroscience at Duke University, can improve decision-making, interactions, relationships, and organizational and societal progress. "Being more attentive to the accuracy of one's views and more open to new information and alternative viewpoints should increase the likelihood that people's beliefs will be based on stronger, more balanced, and more nuanced evidence," Mark writes in an essay.[18]

Like a growth mindset, intellectual humility that expressly welcomes outside perspectives may make leaders more coachable. It also may make them better leaders. Inviting and perhaps adopting employee ideas—especially if those opinions differ from the leader's—indicate a significant measure of respect. Consequently, it contributes to both better decisions and higher morale.

A coach was working with Ron, a start-up entrepreneur, who chafed between his stated desire to get his team to take more ownership and his innate desire to always be the smartest person in the room. In Ron's view, he alone had the right answer to any given problem. No one else could come up with it. "Prove that to me," his coach told him. "Try not having the answer at the next meeting. Just tell me that they all stumbled around in the dark, and we'll know you were right."

At the next meeting, Ron announced that he would not be coming up with the answers and that his job was to help the team do so. "He assumed it would go poorly," she says. "But thirty-five minutes later they had come up with more and better answers than he alone would have." Astonished, Ron reported back to the coach. "You know," he told her, "I think I may have been wrong."

Who else is great at receiving input? Coaches. No one understands better the value that input provides. No one knows better how to catalyze it for measurable improvement. But the close relationship that makes a leader-coach partnership so productive can get in the way, and it can make it hard for the leader to provide the coach with constructive criticism if and when the time comes. "It takes a long time before clients are ready to give that feedback to their coach," says David Noble. "And the deep stuff? Things like, 'You totally missed the mark.' 'You did not get me.' 'You are not listening.' That is very hard to solicit."

One coach was working with a leader who had trouble giving candid feedback. As an experiment, she called her client and asked that he give her feedback in the manner she had been urging him to adopt with his team. "He couldn't do it," says the coach. "I said to him, 'You have got to be able to do it. I am asking for it.' He told me, 'I think it is going really, really, really well.'"

"No," the coach replied. "That is the problem exactly."

While producing feedback might take a back seat to receiving it, all players in the input process matter. Extend and expand that to your life as a whole, and you are well on your way to becoming a better leader and a better human.

A MOMENT WITH MARSHALL:
OPEN TO FEEDBACK

I first met Alan Mulally when he was the CEO of Boeing Commercial Airplanes. He and his team successfully navigated the September 11 attacks, one of the most damaging moments in commercial aviation history. Upon leaving Boeing, Alan became the CEO of Ford. He led the company to one of the most remarkable turnarounds in the history of business. Considered by many to be one of the top five CEOs of all time, Alan is humble and unassuming. He is also precise, practical, and driven to do the right thing in business and life. He is an engineer by training, which showed in everything he did. One attribute that makes Alan exceptional is that he is always open to new challenges and willing to take and act on any advice that he thinks will make him or the company he works for better.

During our first meeting, he and I discussed his tenure at Boeing, including the celebratory wins in addition to the challenges he was facing. We discussed how he was being called on to expand his contribution from leading Commercial Airplanes to playing an even larger role in influencing the entire company. From the beginning, Alan was clearly a great leader who wanted to make an even larger contribution!

In about one hour, I described the Stakeholder-Centered Coaching process to Alan. As it turned out, this process was very aligned to what he was already doing as a leader.

After my thorough description of Stakeholder-Centered Coaching, including the steps involved and the results that followed, Alan smiled and said, "Is that all there is to this process?"

I replied, "That's about it!"

Alan then said something very profound, "Marshall, we are responsible for building planes with over four million parts. We have zero tolerance for failure because we are responsible for people's lives. Following your guidance is the least I can do." And then he did.

As we continued to touch base, Alan also provided me with one of the most important pieces of feedback I have received. "Marshall," he said, "here is something I've learned in business. It is my number one rule. To get great outputs, you must start with great inputs. Client selection is the most important part of your business."

After Alan became the CEO of Ford, we revisited this conversation. He gave me some very profound advice that both changed my life and ultimately changed the field of coaching: "Your greatest challenge as a coach is client selection. If you work with great leaders, who are highly motivated to keep becoming even better, the Stakeholder-Centered Coaching process will always work. If you work with leaders who are not truly committed, the process will never work."

Alan then added, "Never make the coaching process about yourself, your own ego, and how smart you think you are. Make it about the great leaders you serve and how proud you are of them."

Alan next explained how this same philosophy permeated his view of leadership. He said, "As the CEO of Ford, my job is not that different. I do not design the cars. I do not build the cars. I do not sell the cars. I just have to work with great people!" He then added, "For individual achievers, success may be 'all about me.' For great leaders, success is 'all about them.'"

Alan's comments indicate why he was both a fantastic coaching client and an amazing leader! If you are a potential coaching client, please remember Alan's words. The most important variable for success in the coaching relationship is not the coach, it is YOU, the person who is being coached.

EXECUTIVE SUMMARY
Foundations of Feedback

Leadership is an ever-evolving proposition, morphing through many changes in the past century. Its goalposts are constantly moving, so leaders must adapt accordingly; feedback is key to successful adaptation.

- **Identify your blind spots.** Identifying blind spots is essential for moving forward. We all have them, whether they arise from unconscious biases or from unhelpful behaviors. Discovering a blind spot often yields immediate results.
- **Welcome feedback.** Good leaders must welcome feedback. It is not enough to merely feel open to feedback. You must

also convince those providing feedback that you desire it. Offer no judgment—just say "thank you" each time. Treat feedback as the precious gift that it is.

- **Separate the good feedback from the bad.** Be on the lookout for toxic or unhelpful feedback. Try to separate the wheat from the chaff.
- **Embrace intellectual humility.** A primary quality for successful leadership is intellectual humility. Great leaders recognize that they can be wrong, and they accept the moments that they fall short as truth.

Learn from Alan Mulally's great example: The most important variable for success in coaching is you, a great client!

CHAPTER SIX

OPEN TO TAKING ACTION

FROM UNDERSTANDING TO ACTION

Becoming coachable means being open to taking action. Real action, in the real world. If we think of science for a moment, we can easily identify two main types of pursuit: theoretical and applied. Theoretical science seeks to advance pure knowledge. Applied science uses that knowledge to make a difference in the world.

The same holds true for leadership knowledge. You understand the model of exceptional leadership your coach and stakeholders envisage for you. You agree with their suggestions for achieving it. But those conditions are not sufficient. Analysis can lead to paralysis. "Openness to action is never enough," says Michelle Tillis Lederman. "You've got to commit to taking action."

The mandate to act often is where a leader's uncoachability first surfaces. It is easy to profess openness to change when talking to your coach. When those 360 results come back, after an initial grimace, you likely will choke out an acceptance of the criticisms voiced. But then, when you are required to do something—a scary something—that will take monumental time and effort, change suddenly becomes a little too real. There's a reason that, in many instances, the status quo is comfortable.

"People think talking about how they show up is equivalent to actually changing how they show up," says Whitney Johnson. "They are not even aware that they are unwilling to do the work."

Bruce, an entrepreneur, really wanted to change. He wanted to improve his relationship with his business partner, and he enlisted a coach to support him. Bruce was a great business partner when the two were fully aligned. But each time his business partner began to make a decision that differed from his, Bruce would step in, take over her work, and essentially strong-arm her into doing things his preferred way. Each week, his coach reminded him of his intention, and each week he renewed his pledge. But when the situation arose, he continued allowing his emotions to get the best of him and returned to the same old rut. His coach gave him an ultimatum: "I can't be your coach if you aren't willing to do the hard work of change. I don't want to waste your time and mine." Ultimately, Bruce was resolute in doing things his way. He decided that he wasn't yet ready to be coached.

Coaching is not just about understanding what is important to you and why. Nor does it encourage you to develop skills in a vacuum. Even as you absorb the lessons of coaching, you must put them into practice. By the end of six months, you should be observing concrete, measurable improvements in your performance and your work relationships. Your bosses, colleagues, and reports should begin noticing them, too.

So long as you are open to change and open to input, you also should be open to—and embrace—action. But taking action usually involves other people. You will have to have difficult conversations. You will probably need to do some things you've been putting off. You may need to reach out to colleagues you do not like or trust. As a leader, you almost certainly will have to pay closer attention to your team and prioritize their needs.

And, complicating matters, people rarely react the way you think they will. Among coaching's greatest gifts is that it stiffens your spine and prepares you to deal with unpredictable situations. Yet, in the moment, things can get unpleasant. Most of the folks you are talking to and enacting change with are not being coached. You are coming to them armed with new skills and perspectives. Most will respond from their same old playbooks.

Many leaders have observed that while action is difficult, inaction is not an option. If you harbor some vague idea that intention is sufficient—that you can change on the inside without expressing that change on the outside—a coach will disabuse you of that notion quickly. They will make sure you follow through on your commitments. In addition to motivating, coaches are good at nudging you forward.

Your coach will give you permission to do things you are already motivated to do, a permission you may not be willing to give yourself because the action feels too risky. Having someone in your corner will make it easier to go ahead and give yourself that permission to take action that improves yourself, your organization, and the people around you.

Miranda, a senior vice president at a defense contractor, was unhappy with both her compensation and the priorities being set for her. Every session, she and her coach talked about it.

They role-played the conversation she wanted to have with her boss. Meanwhile, Miranda tried mustering her courage and discipline. "I would ask, 'Are you ready to do it?' She would say, 'I'm not ready,'" says the coach. "A month goes by. 'Are you ready to do it?' 'I'm not ready.' A month goes by. 'Are you ready to do it?' 'I think I'm ready.'"

Miranda and the coach practiced some more. Then Miranda talked to her boss. The boss would not give her what she wanted. So, she found a much better job and left the company. "It was beautiful," says the coach, "because she walked away knowing she had done it."

Perhaps most important of all, your coach will help you formulate a plan. Action without planning rarely produces the desired outcome. Sometimes, it is downright counterproductive.

Doing what you do not want to do is difficult. A great coach will make sure you do it and do it right. In fact, hiring a coach is a form of action. So, you have already begun to get moving.

INSTILLING THE WILL TO ACT

Executive coaches motivate leaders to take action. They do so chiefly by igniting "intrinsic" motivation: a leader's personal, deeply felt reason for doing something. Compared with extrinsic motivation—which relies on such external rewards as a higher salary—intrinsic motivation produces greater persistence, deeper engagement, and overall better outcomes, research shows.[19, 20] Oftentimes, it carries parallel rewards that speak to the leader's extrinsic motivations—which, it should be noted, are often equally important—as well.

One coach recalls being part of a workshop in a large company where high potentials were being coached. Emmanuel, a young up-and-comer, was laboring over a writing exercise related to coaching. "I told him he looked like they were making him eat coal and asked what the story was," says the coach. Emmanuel told her he was supposed to work on his stakeholder management and found it mind-deadening.

The coach saw an opportunity to ignite Emmanuel's intrinsic motivation. She said, "Let's forget about that for a minute. What do you actually want to do? What is your goal in life?" He told her he wanted to return to his home country, join the cabinet, and help run the government. The coach asked whether practicing stakeholder management might help him achieve that dream. "He came alive and practically pushed me out of the way to start working," says the coach. This is an example of how reframing a problem, question, or prompt can inspire engagement by the leader and, ultimately, lead to action down the road.

Ask a coach what constitutes a red flag in a new client. Often, they will mention a statement like, "My board/boss is making me do this. Personally, I don't see the point."

Dean Miles says that about a third of his clients will come in with a list of things they want to work on and a desire to follow their curiosity. Another third reserve judgment but are intrigued. Then there are the hard cases. "They say, 'Are we going to do trust falls? Are we going to hug it out? How much is the company spending on this waste of time?'" says Dean. "Their arms are crossed over their chests. There is a lot of vulgar language."

Charlie, a director of an art consortium, had been pushed into coaching by his boss. He procrastinated six months before setting up a meeting with a coach. "Our very first time together, he taps his watch and says, 'How long is this going to take?'" recalls the coach. She replied, "I believe coaching should fit into the time frame and the needs of the client, not the other way around. If we have a conversation, what would be useful to you?" The switch in focus from compliance with his boss's desires to fulfillment of Charlie's own desires kick-started their relationship.

When a leader tells Carol Kauffman they want to try something that came up in a coaching session, Carol will say, "Great. On a scale of one to ten, how motivated are you to try this?" Anything less than eight, she says, "is not going to happen. Because we have got a million things crowding that out. So, let's try something else."

Say the leader's motivation is at a nine or ten. The next question is then: "How confident are you that you actually will do this?" That prods the leader to get real about the commitment. If their confidence level is not high, then Carol suggests that they try shrinking the target to something that at least gets the leader moving toward the goal.

Sometimes, neither extrinsic nor intrinsic motivations are enough. You may be intrigued by the idea of being coached. But for some reason—not because you're too busy, not because you think it won't work—coaching just is not the best thing for you at a particular moment in time. That is okay.

Beth Polish recently demurred from working with a high-potential leader whose boss wanted coaching for him. The high-potential wanted coaching but thought he was not ready for it. "I said not to push it," says Beth. "He's not coachable if he doesn't think this is the right time. We can come back to it."

ROLE-PLAYING WITH YOUR COACH

Now comes the fun part. You get to playact. Before you take real action, you get to be the star of your own show and take a bow.

A whole swath of coaching targets public speaking, a fear that haunts many of us. It is hardly a surprise that a vision of a podium, a microphone, and a stone-faced crowd sends knees quaking. A coach can help you workshop that career-making presentation and generally improve your executive presence and flair on the dais.

But the public does not talk back, at least at well-behaved gatherings. How much more unnerving, then, are difficult one-on-one conversations, such as those leading to firing an employee or demanding a raise or confronting a colleague who has been falling down on a project? Upset or challenged people are unpredictable. You can't control their responses. Unsurprisingly, leaders often postpone such conversations or never have the talk at all.

Coaches will not let you get away with that avoidance. They are like your dogged, six-in-the-morning personal trainer when you are hungover. They will make you practice and practice and practice that interaction until you have mastered what to say, how to say it, and how to field every possible riposte from the other person. Then the coach will check in with you over and over until you report that you have had the dreaded conversation. This persistence may sound miserable. In reality, it's supportive and, ultimately, liberating.

Coaches use role-playing to get you comfortable with an action. The coach plays you, and you play one of your reports. That way you see, from the other person's perspective, what the exchange looks like. Then you switch it up. "After you've practiced, then you apply it in the real world," says John Reed. "You can learn how to ride English style. But until you get on the horse, it is an abstraction."

Coaches will also lead you through contingency planning, so you do not go into battle with a lone arrow in your quiver. If such-and-such happens, what will you do? How about if so-and-so replies with an answer from left field? "You want to be prepared with four or more ways to win," says David Noble. "Inevitably, you are going to face obstacles and curveballs."

Dean Miles warns coached leaders to prepare to be annoyed. When coaching someone for a challenging encounter, "I'll ask them, 'What are you going to say?'" says Dean. "They'll say it. And I'll say, 'That was terrible. Terrible.' It doesn't matter if it was or it wasn't. I'm trying to shock them. To get them to change perspectives. 'How else could you say it? How else? Do it again. Again.'"

Dean adds, "It's extremely aggravating. But that's where the growth comes. Your coach is your greatest advocate and the biggest pain in the rear you have ever experienced."

Behavioral exercise is like physical exercise: The goal is to build muscle. That means you need to take every opportunity to try out your new behaviors. You'll have to create opportunities if they don't present themselves.

Alas, practice isn't enough. Bringing down the temperature on long-bubbling tensions or heated conflicts requires emotional courage, a topic that Peter Bregman describes in his bestselling book *Leading with Emotional Courage: How to Have Hard Conversations, Create Accountability, and Inspire Action on Your Most Important Work*. Probably at this moment there is a difficult conversation you are avoiding, even though you have had plenty of opportunities to initiate it and know everything necessary to conduct it. Peter Bregman says the reason for such procrastination is simple: fear of feeling something. "You might feel shame or worry about hurting them or about risking the relationship," says Peter. "If you are willing to feel everything, then you can do anything."

We have said earlier that coaching can be an uncomfortable experience. Being nudged into these dicey conversations will likely constitute the most challenging piece of your coaching engagement. In addition to demanding emotional courage, they will require a degree of consideration, perspective, and control that is often hard to sustain. These qualities are all muscles that you will need to build. When you have finally resolved the conflict, you can learn from it and move forward with newfound confidence.

ON DISCIPLINE AND TIME NEEDED

The work begins with planning. As we discussed when speaking of baby steps, planning starts with identifying one or two areas targeted for improvement. You should prioritize behaviors that are well-defined and measurable.

Sometimes, a leader will propose a target behavior that is too vague. Michelle Tillis Lederman will ask a leader, "How do I know you did that? How do *you* know?" She will press the leader on what specific actions they will take. "Are you going to give feedback to more people or more often? Are you going to make sure your feedback starts with a positive comment?"

A coach will work with you to create some kind of written development plan that spells out items such as actions, time frames, expected outcomes, and metrics for accomplishment. It may also prompt you to anticipate problems along the way. Sometimes, the plan will help you identify discrete actions that advance a narrow goal in the context of your broader career trajectory. This is eyes-on-the-prize stuff. You are balancing skill development with goal setting. Michelle suggests always keeping your plan close at hand, in plain sight.

You may want to run your plan by your boss to ensure the goals are in line with the company's intentions for you. Your boss's awareness of what you are trying to accomplish and your progress toward that goal may even affect your performance reviews. Consider the latter an extrinsic side dish of motivation, which makes purposeful action all the more rewarding.

Much of the hard work will take place in the days between weekly meetings with your coach. That is when clients try out their new skills in the unprotected, unpredictable workplace. Without a coach demanding their focus, leaders must remember what they have learned and intentionally bring it into play. They must do what they have committed to do and be who they are striving to be at every moment. If they don't, their coach will soon figure it out.

"This is where you are moving from an abstract into practice," says Nilofer Merchant. Nilofer asks leaders to keep a daily journal of their actions. She will weigh in with a question every two or three days to keep the key principles in their heads to "enhance their cycle of observation and practice," she says.

Breaking big jobs into multiple small tasks can curb procrastination. If checklists motivate you to get moving, then you may want to compile one every week or so. You should be able to say, "I'm going to perform this action now." Then do it. Then give yourself a check. Then report back to your coach. And then, you need to do that again and again.

David Noble says leaders often will experience a flash of insight or an "embodied moment" in which they realize that change really is happening. That provides the motivation to keep going. "After that, it's all about the repetitions," David says. "If you do it enough, then it becomes part of your routine. Then you can work on something else."

Leaders should place that motto—"It's all about the repetitions"—on their computer screen saver. Meaningful action requires repetition. But repetition requires discipline. And discipline means you keep doing something even when it is hard. For leaders, working on things they expect to pay off in the future is difficult when, in their work life, they are grappling with things that must get done in the present. That is a fact of life, so they must be prepared to juggle.

We often think of taking action as something we instigate on our own. Such an opinion stems from what may be called the myth of self-sufficiency, when, in fact, coaching a leader is a team sport. Your coworkers will do what they can to advance the process. It is in their best interest that you succeed.

Let's say a leader recognizes that he has anger issues. He commits with his coach to conquering those issues and says to his stakeholders that he is working on taming his anger. Then days later he flies off the handle and rips into his subordinates repeatedly. The intention was there, but not the action. The fellow should go back to the drawing board with his coach and try again. Although many leaders crave instant results, the process of taking action is a lengthy street with many potholes along the way.

NOT ALL ACTION IS GOOD

We have arrived at yet another section that you might construe as waffling about our overall message. But, we want to recognize the complexity of coaching at every turn. And, in this moment, it's important to recognize that taking action and putting yourself out there can have its downsides. It's important for both the leader and the coach to weigh each goal and action item and prioritize those in which the upside outweighs any associated downsides (if there are any).

As we mentioned before, in coaching there are no absolutes. However, this is an unequivocal truth: At times, doing nothing is better than doing something.

Students of boxing history will no doubt know of the famous 1974 bout that took place in Kinshasa, Zaire, between Muhammad Ali and then-heavyweight champion George Foreman. It was dubbed "The Rumble in the Jungle." As one-quarter of the world's population watched on television, Ali stunned everyone by doing nothing. He leaned back on the ropes for several rounds, his gloves protecting his head, and let Foreman land punch after sledgehammer punch to his body. Foreman could not have known that Ali had undertaken intense physical training in the months leading up to the fight that had rendered his abs as hard as titanium. Mere body blows, even from the mighty Foreman, could not fell him.

This tactic, known as "rope-a-dope" in boxing circles, eventually tired the reigning champ. Foreman landed hundreds of punches, and Ali did not flinch. After the sixth round, Ali saw that Foreman was well and truly exhausted. He went on the offensive, pummeling the wobbly Foreman with repeated right hooks to the head. Ali won by a knockout in the eighth round.

His initial inaction had clinched the outcome of the fight. To repeat: Sometimes doing nothing trumps taking action.

Granted, the client being coached will not have a round in the ring to endure. Conference-room squabbling, however testy, seldom entails the throwing of haymakers. But the "rope-a-dope" tactic can be useful to adapt and keep in mind.

Nilofer Merchant recalls coaching a high-flying client who put his name forward for a very senior position. He did not get it; instead, recruiters selected a colleague with a different vision. Her client's fortunes took a turn when the successful candidate left the position a mere six months later. Senior management urged him to try again.

She pleaded with him: Don't do it. Hang back and wait. If you accept an offer and then have to adopt your rival's vision of the job, you will be miserable. Let them come to you—classic rope-a-dope. In time, management did come to him and pleaded with him to reapply for the job. No, he replied. I will do so only if you let me execute my vision, not my predecessor's. Eventually senior management reevaluated the situation and aligned with his vision, awarding Nilofer's client the position and allowing the scope and role to be what he was best suited for. He had won by doing squat—a calculated nothing. And the bet paid off. Sometimes the best action is the intentional choice of no action at all.

Lest people think we are pandering here to the stick-in-the mud old guard, we ask them to consider the words of Greta Thunberg, global climate activist. A member of Gen Z, the outspoken Greta is known as an advocate of action, but even she is wary of *all* action. As she writes in *No One Is Too Small to Make a Difference:* "Sometimes NOT doing things—like just sitting down outside the parliament—speaks much louder than doing things. Just like a whisper sometimes is louder than shouting."

A MOMENT WITH MARSHALL:
OPEN TO ACTION

When I was a doctoral candidate at UCLA, I hurt my middle finger while playing basketball. A medical-school friend thought the injury was something called "baseball finger." I looked it up and read about the treatment. I would need to wear a splint at all times for eight weeks. I had to—very carefully—wash and dry the finger on a flat surface. If I bent it even a tiny bit, then I might stretch the tendon and would have to start the process all over.

Still, I went to the university medical center to have a doctor take a look. When I told him what I suspected and about the therapy, he agreed with it. He told me to follow the instructions for splinting and washing and come back in eight weeks. When I returned, I was able to assure the doctor that I had followed the instructions to a T. He was shocked: more so when he examined my finger and discovered it had completely healed. "Almost nobody ever does this for eight weeks!" he told me. "I am amazed that you actually did all of that stuff."

You can correctly diagnose a problem in your leadership or your life. You can know the actions that will fix that problem. But that knowledge is useless if you don't do the work. If you don't exercise the skills. If you don't give your reports space to question you, or clearly communicate to people what is expected of them, or speak calmly when someone misses a deadline and you feel like yelling your head off.

Positive, long-term change requires that you take actions—over and over and over—to build the muscle and, over time, heal any injuries you may have done to yourself or others. Like therapy for baseball finger, your instructions will be easy. Carrying them out with unswerving discipline will be hard. Sometimes, very hard. But if you are serious about harnessing intentional action to inspire change, you can do it.

EXECUTIVE SUMMARY
All About Taking Action

Understanding that an action is called for does not replace actually *taking* action. One must make moves when appropriate and thought-out, not just talk about said moves with a coach. Before you take that leap, there are a variety of factors to consider.

- **Look to intrinsic drivers for motivation.** Meaningful action requires repetition. And repetition requires discipline. While extrinsic drivers, such as hopes of promotion or higher salary, are important, intrinsic drivers, such as the desire to positively influence your team, generally lead to more effective action.
- **Plan before you act.** Taking action requires careful planning. Your coach can help with this.
- **Develop a detailed action plan.** A coach will collaborate with you to craft a detailed development plan, outlining actions, timelines, projected outcomes, and achievement metrics. Implementing this plan requires dedication and a commitment to invest the necessary time.

- **Rehearse before acting.** It is not uncommon to role-play with a coach before taking action, be it finally having that tough conversation or public speaking in a high-pressure environment.
- **Decide whether or not to act.** In some instances, doing nothing is better than doing something. Before you press ahead, carefully assess the situation.

Well planned action has the power to move mountains, in an organization and beyond.

CHAPTER SEVEN

OPEN TO ACCOUNTABILITY

We hope that, thus far, you have gotten a good sense of what you need to bring to a coaching engagement to maximize its efficacy.

If you're still with us, we assume you are open to inviting change, welcoming feedback, and taking action. And while that seems like the full package, there is one more element that you must commit to in order to create *lasting* change: embracing accountability. Too many of the great things you gain from coaching will not stick if you are not held accountable. Coaching engagements typically last six months to a year, and during that time your coach will be your key accountability partner. Real behavior change may take longer than that. And, unfortunately, good habits are often broken more easily than bad ones. So, you must be willing to be open to accountability before, during, and after the coaching engagement. Let's consider why.

THE BACKSLIDING TEMPTATION

There is change. Then there is lasting change. Lasting change is the kind that matters. Some people may want to believe that simply having had a coach makes them immune to future failures. While coaching gives you tools to help prevent bad habits from returning, it's you who has to exercise those tools regularly to ensure you stay in good practice.

Marshall's classic study, "Leadership is a Contact Sport," established the bar. His summary says it all: "If the organization can teach the leader to reach out to coworkers, to listen and learn, and to focus on continuous development, both the leader and the organization will benefit. After all, by following up with colleagues, a leader demonstrates a commitment to self-improvement—and a determination to get better. This process does not have to take a lot of time or money. There's something far more valuable: contact." By publicly holding yourself accountable, you not only reinforce your positive gains, but you also demonstrate your willingness to grow and set an example for others to follow. And in the process, you are continuing to shepherd the greatest shift of all: the perception of others.

Accountability comes in many forms, including external and internal. The key is to ensure you have proactive external accountability through the feedback of bosses, peers, friends, and family. Let them know that you want the feedback to continue. Relying wholly on internal drive and motivation can lead you down a hall of mirrors, where you no longer know which direction you should be going (isn't that part of what caused you to hire a coach in the first place?).

Research suggests that motivation is a finite resource, and we only have a limited quantity each day, usually a smaller amount than we think.[21] But most of us do find the external alarms and reminders of others to be highly motivating (as in an email from your boss with the subject line "Urgent"). Accountability is a lot like that; it is motivating. As with feedback, accountability is a gift. It means someone cares about you and wants to help you grow. And, as we also recommend with feedback, the best response when someone gives accountability pointers is "thank you." We all need accountability, especially leaders. We all recognize that great leaders are people who take responsibility. Part of responsibility is accountability.

With feedback, you want to know what you *should* be doing. With accountability, you want to know *how well* you are doing the things you've identified as important; the things you've promised to others with respect to your growth and development. The fact that you have willingly asked for it does not make it easier. When people give you feedback, they may or may not believe that you will improve. When they hold you accountable, they find out the degree to which they were right about you.

Feedback is about identification. Other people give their opinions on what you should do. That can be humbling. Accountability is about execution and consistency. You ask your coach or an accountability partner to hold you to the commitments that you chose, and you may feel exposed in the process. With feedback, you can consciously or unconsciously make excuses or write it off as an uninformed opinion. Accountability isn't like that; ultimately, there's no one to blame but yourself.

Another point in common: You may not enjoy listening to someone who is delivering feedback. Similarly, you may not want to talk to someone who is holding you accountable. If you have been meticulously practicing your new behaviors and pursuing your goals, then a positive assessment will be yours to enjoy. But if you have fallen off the wagon, you probably will not want to be called out on it. And most of us will know the precise moment that we fell.

In more eloquent terms, we refer to this as a backslide. It happens frequently, and we're all susceptible to them, no matter how coachable we become. Let's say the coach is no longer there to nudge and encourage you in the right direction. You may have learned a good habit from that coach, but you practiced it only in a certain context. Perhaps the context changes or your environment changes, and the habit becomes much harder to sustain. "Habits depend on cues and environmental guardrails," says leadership coach Caroline Webb. "So, it is very likely that when you stop working with your coach, there will be backsliding. You would not be human if you did not see your behavior revert a little bit."

In time, you will also become more vulnerable to the relentless pressure of the here and now since a coach often serves as an accountability partner. It is up to you to enlist and enroll new accountability partners once your time with your coach is up. People are wired to focus on problems with immediate, certain consequences rather than on those with future, uncertain ones, according to Harvard psychologist Daniel Gilbert, who has written about this phenomenon as it relates to the non-urgency of our response to climate change.[22]

Coaching brings immediacy to long-term problems with leadership skills, prompting you to address the problems now. Let's say the glitch lies in an inability to listen. This was one of the behaviors you and your coach decided to work on. Consequently, while you are being coached, having three impending deadlines should not prevent you from making the time to listen with patience and empathy to at least one person a day. When your coach vanishes at the end of the engagement, those deadlines roar back in your ears. Listening can drop to the bottom of your to-do list.

Some falloff is normal. Yet, if you set up accountability systems before your coaching engagement concludes, then you should be able to sustain and build on the important work you have accomplished. As it is happening, that engagement always includes accountability, long before you and your coach part ways.

During his coaching, Brian, an executive of a financial services firm, grew less gruff, more patient, and less likely to lash out. His colleagues noticed. They sent him congratulatory emails, which he proudly shared with his coach. But the same stakeholders reserved judgment. They were suspicious that his better behavior might be temporary—that it was a result of what is called "the coaching bump." When the engagement was over, Brian did nothing to make his new behaviors permanent. Sure enough, "Now I hear he is inconsistent with the learned skill," says the coach with a sigh. "As a result, trust has started to erode."

Listen, we all need accountability. For the past two decades, Marshall has been coaching and teaching others to adopt what he calls "Daily Questions," a set of questions we ask ourselves each day to hold ourselves accountable to our goals. The participant writes *both* the questions and the answers. The impact and insight rendered from this process are staggering. Still, Marshall has someone call him every day. Why? Because the hardest part of holding yourself accountable is finding the internal motivation to do so.

Demanding perfection of yourself, by yourself, guarantees failure. To permanently embed the behaviors learned in coaching, you must practice them over and over. Leaders must do their best not to deviate from their intent, not to fall short for even a day. This sounds impossible, and it is. Deviation will occur, and progress will be set back. The best thing to do then is to report it, honestly, to yourself and to your colleagues. You are all in this together.

We get it—feedback and accountability are hard. If it were easy, everyone would be doing it. Feedback and accountability can also be uncomfortable. Part of working with a coach is to help you to become more comfortable with the process. This will not rid you of all discomfort; it's still hard work, and people can be harsh. After all, not everyone is skilled at providing feedback or accountability, but you'll need to forgive them for that and thank them anyway. At the end of the day, discomfort is a sure sign of growth, and that's what we're after.

PROGRESS AND PERCEPTION

"To grow as a leader at all levels, you must be able to see the situation from other people's perspective," says one of our coaches. "Knowing what's important to them is an essential ingredient for successful leadership. It's *me* in the context of *we*."

Reporting back to your coach every couple of weeks during the entire duration of the engagement will keep you accountable for acting on your commitments. Our emphasis here is on the progress the leader is making along with the perception of their progress in the workplace. The two are intertwined.

The knowledge that you have to report your actions to your coach down the line may also hold you accountable to pay close attention in each actionable moment. If you rush through an action to get it over with, then you may fail to see signals from others that will help you understand what happened. You also may forget what you said or how you said it, making it difficult to improve your performance. Knowing that you'll have to report the process of a particular action after the fact can keep you more present in any given moment.

Beth Polish treats reporting sessions like after-action reviews, deconstructing everything about a meeting or interaction, from the setup of the room where the meeting took place to any informal conversation before the central exchange. "I want to know what the other person really said. Did you ask what their thinking was? What follow-up question do you wish you had asked? What's the worst thing that would have happened if you had?" Beth says that when leaders take stock of their actions, it is important for them to fully understand why things unfolded as they did. Otherwise, "You may keep ruminating and ruminating on it," she says. "And the effect of that can be terrible."

During these accountability reporting sessions, leaders mentally compile with their coach what David Noble calls "the user's manual to you." It takes a while to unpack all the micro-behaviors that affect your ability to achieve and sustain change. "Most people can't sit with their feelings for five seconds," says David. "It's really hard to sit for an hour while someone is asking, 'And then what happened? And why did you do that?' You need the right relationship to support that exploration."

Despite all the effort required, you'll need to ensure accountability does not become a burden. It's akin to a dieter's bathroom scale—though it may be a tool to reassure yourself of progress, it can become a toxic obsession very quickly. So much so, that the dieter may lose sight of why they started the journey in the first place—to become healthier, not to hit an abstract number on the scale.

Progress is something we understand: It's a process of betterment that passes through multiple stages. Perception of progress is less straightforward. The opinions of others are out of the leader's hands. Yet leaders may nonetheless exercise some influence on these perceptions if they make sure to communicate clearly and repeatedly to their colleagues what they are attempting—and, most important, if they hold themselves accountable to these same colleagues for whatever failures and successes have transpired. Coach Alex Lazarus advises that leaders need to understand the specific communication style needs of each of their reports in order to be their most effective. Leaders should do this explicitly, without window dressing. Following up with stakeholders keeps you committed. But it also reminds those you work with that you are committed. They will give you brownie points for that.

Let's take hypothetical examples about why follow-up accountability is important. For this example, we will return to the well of destructive comments and anger. This character trait is the starkest and, in many ways, the easiest to see. Bright colors attract attention. Hence our use of these flaws in constructing an instructive hypothetical situation.

Let's say your stakeholders claim that you are a gold medalist when it comes to making destructive comments. Difficult to fix, but doable: You must simply stop making destructive comments. You say you are working on that and will soon be doing great.

Your coaching may be over, so you and your stakeholders may be on your own. Then, and here is where accountability comes in, you do one of two things:

Case A: After the initial feedback, you go to your stakeholders, thank them for their input, and ask for their ideas about eliminating your propensity for snide and negative commentary. But that is the last time you bring up the subject with them. Seven months pass, and you do not make a single destructive comment. Well done. Then one day, you lose it. "Those stupid idiots in finance!" you yell. "Dumb bean counters! How can I get anything done when I'm surrounded by people like this?" One of your colleagues who participated in your 360 overhears this tirade. That single outburst triggers his previous conception of you. You have not changed. Still the same old hothead.

Case B: This scenario begins in the same manner: After the initial feedback, you go to your stakeholders, thank them for their input, and ask for their ideas. But in this case, two months later you go back to them. You repeat what you said in your first session: that you want to be a team player and are trying not to make destructive comments. You ask for more ideas. Your stakeholders may reply, "You know what? You have been doing better. Keep it up." Two months later: same thing. Two months after that: same thing. At seven months, however, the kettle starts its ear-splitting whistle: "Those stupid idiots in finance!" In this second scenario, the colleague who witnesses the tantrum, says, "You know, you really should not say that. But you went for months without insulting anyone. Clearly you are making progress."

In Case A, did your behavior change? Yes. Did your colleague's perception of you change? No. In Case B, both the behavior and the perception changed. In leadership, what you say matters less than what they hear. If you do not follow up assiduously in acknowledging accountability, even if your behavior changes, the perceptions of your colleagues may stay the same.

After your colleague remarks on your progress, you could thank him and apologize. If your comments get back to the people you were in the process of insulting, perhaps apologize to them as well.

WHO CAN CALL ME OUT?

If you want your stakeholders to credit your improvement, you can follow up with them every two months for the duration of your coaching. But what happens after the engagement ends? You can tie a ribbon around yourself and proclaim that you are the complete package. But chances are, with no one holding you accountable, you are going to backslide.

To prevent that, you can try to hold yourself accountable. However, keeping yourself honest takes tremendous discipline. After all, you are probably the only person who understands the extraordinary circumstances that led you to trip up that last time. Naturally, you will be tempted to give yourself a pass. Next week will be better. No question.

Instead of performing the difficult feat of flying solo, we recommend that you seek out what we call accountability partners. These are people you check in with regularly, people whose opinions and feedback you respect. For very senior executives, these partners are usually senior peers themselves. That way, you can avoid possible power imbalances. When, say, a C-suite denizen approaches a more junior employee for input, that person may be reluctant to speak their mind freely, out of natural hierarchical deference. A peer partner faces no such obstacle. And if these partners have themselves been coached, so much the better.

Let's use the sports metaphor again. Your coach is like your personal trainer. They hold you accountable to come to the gym every week. After all, they will know if you don't show up, and you are paying for their time and services regardless. Accountability makes you show up, and its motivation pushes you to work a little harder, dig a little deeper, reach a little higher. And the coach's knowledge and even-keeled observations give you the confidence and psychological safety to do so.

After six months or a year of working with a personal trainer, some people decide to move on. Generally, one of three things then happens. Some people have the value of health and exercise deeply instilled in them and are able to mostly adhere to their commitment of regular exercise. We say "mostly" because some backsliding is almost always inevitable. Other people can enlist a partner or friend to be their workout buddy. Together, they hold one another accountable to their goal of regular exercise. And still others try to go it alone (what we called earlier "flying solo") before realizing how difficult it is to stay motivated. Alas, they eventually find themselves at a similar place from which they started. Many of these people return to their personal trainer and commit to working together on an ongoing basis. And that's fine. There is nothing wrong with having a personal trainer. We're all human. We all need help. We all need accountability.

At this juncture, readers who may have sighed at our repeated emphasis on the shortcomings of leaders will be relieved to hear that not everything is their fault. Backsliding that cries out for accountability can occur throughout an organization. As the permission-to-speak glow created by the coaching engagement begins to dim, there is a danger that colleagues and subordinates may revert to the bad old days of keeping their heads down and clamming up. The leader is still the leader, after all. Some stakeholders may grow cagey about providing honest feedback.

Your accountability partner can help fill that gap. You can further improve the odds of getting sustained feedback if you hire or develop people whose accountability roles are understood as part of their job description. A founder-CEO, for example, "could hire a great second in command, who isn't afraid to call them out," says Alisa Cohn. Or maybe a manager is brought in to handle those tasks at which a leader does not excel. Once a leader builds a solid relationship with that person, they may, Alisa says, "become an embedded coach inside the operation."

Accountability partners can come in all flavors. They may be a trusted friend, a close associate, an up-and-coming colleague, or a wise and experienced senior executive. Or perhaps all of the above. You can have as many accountability partners as you want, though you are more likely to lean on just one or two. Too many chefs can spoil the broth, no matter how varied the flavors. Even if you engage just a couple of partners, their input is invaluable in keeping you on track—and on your toes.

NOT ALL ACCOUNTABILITY IS GOOD

This brief section is just a reminder of what you no doubt already know. You must exercise judgment in choosing your obligations. Not all the choices are good. If you are thinking of selecting an accountability partner who you suspect is hiding a dagger behind his back, perhaps think again.

The notion of accountability extends to many aspects of life. A wife of our acquaintance recently sued for divorce. The reason? Accountability. Her husband made an absolute priority of his job, habitually staying late in the office and working weekends. If the boss said jump, he asked how high.

He chose to be unswervingly accountable to his company. The wife came in a very distant second, if ever she was really in the race. To make matters worse, he professed to hate his job. What little time he spent at home often resounded with an operatic aria of grievance about his work and his colleagues.

She still felt love for him, but enough was enough. After fifteen years of being disregarded, she gave him his walking papers. Now the man has a job he detests, no wife, and almost no free time—all because of an absolute sense of accountability to his employer.

In some circles, though, the poor fellow might be regarded as a hero. Writer and entrepreneur Colleen Bordeaux conducted several interviews with topmost executives about their path to rising through the ranks. One CEO was blunt: "No one wants to hear this, but I'm successful because I put work above everything else in my life. It's not possible to get to my position without making the same sacrifices." We will examine such decisions in part three of this book, where we discuss and contrast Striving, People-Pleasing, Rising, and Flourishing as the way forward. The balance of competing demands can be a thorny issue.

Back to the dangers of accountability: This time, the cautionary tale came in over the Internet in 2022. The inimitable CEO of Twitter, Elon Musk, sent a midnight email saying that employees "will need to be extremely hardcore" henceforth. "This will mean," he added, "working long hours at high intensity. Only exceptional performance will constitute a passing grade." This was a real-life echo of our entrepreneur mentioned earlier, who was baffled when his staff deserted the office at a conventionally reasonable hour every evening.[23]

The Internet entered the scene when a Twitter executive, Esther Crawford, triumphantly posted a picture of herself wrapped in a silver sleeping bag and fast asleep on the office floor.[24] Esther had taken the boss at his word. Was she a hard-charger or a sacrificial lamb on the altar of a colossal social media company? As usual, commenters weighed in with disgust or delight. What was certain was that Esther had taken accountability to a new level. All work, no life.

The story has a sad ending. In the next round of layoffs at Twitter in early 2023, Esther got the ax. Presumably, she rolled up her sleeping bag and went home to finally get a good night's sleep. Wagering on absolute accountability turned out to be a bad bet.

Like change, input, and action, accountability calls for a clear-eyed assessment of benefits and downsides. We leave that to you.

THE VIRTUOUS CYCLE

Change, feedback, action, accountability. During and after your coaching engagement, these words remain important. You are not on your own, but one day the coach-whisperer will be gone. Some coaches will write disengagement notes, summarizing what you have worked on together. That gives you something to refer to if the lessons start to grow foggy. And, if you forget them altogether, you always have the coach's number.

We are not here to mandate behaviors that will further success. Those behaviors are ultimately up to you as a leader. We can say that reaching the accountability stage may result in starting up what we call a virtuous cycle. We speak here of a cycle, because it is a recurring process that requires us to constantly reinvent ourselves. Part of accountability is asking the question: Am I doing what I set out to do? Yes or no? Is this still the right question for me? Yes or no? If I circle back into being held accountable, then I'm also receiving input. And if I'm receiving feedback, then I'm open to change. And, in turn, if I'm open to change, then I'm open to taking action. Which means that I will be held accountable for such action, which begins the cycle again. It is more than a process; it is progress.

The point here is that becoming coachable, and in turn, being coached, is not a fixed goal with a clearly delineated finish line. This should not be distressing; it should be exhilarating. Who does not want to continue growing? We all want to matter. We all want to be a force for good. The lure of forward motion is irresistible. You are not running on a hamster wheel; you are continuing to achieve your personal bests in a process that should never end. We are all works in progress.

Jada, a seasoned executive, had recently been promoted to

a C-suite position at a prestigious advertising agency. With an impressive track record, she believed she had reached the pinnacle of her career. However, a conversation with a mentor inspired her to consider the idea that her growth was far from complete.

Encouraged by her mentor's advice, Jada decided to work with an executive coach to develop her leadership skills further. With each coaching session, Jada discovered new aspects of her leadership style that she could refine and untapped strengths that she could cultivate. She began to see herself as constantly evolving, always striving to do her best and be a positive light within her organization.

The thrill of continuous growth became exhilarating for Jada, as she embraced the idea of forward motion. Her team took notice of her renewed passion and commitment, and the positive effects rippled throughout the company. Employee engagement and collaboration increased, leading to increased creativity and business performance.

Still, here's what you may be thinking now: "If I can work with a coach for six months or a year and put in the work and progress, only to backslide to the same bad habit a few months later, why try at all?" To this we say, you have still made progress. The results are real—for yourself, the people around you, and your company. But no matter how far we have come, the journey does not get easier. We have to keep doing the work. Leadership is not for the faint of heart. And because you have had a coach, you know the path to growth. You know the training exercises. You can do it. Keep going. And enlist support along the way as needed. Even if you're no longer working together in a paid capacity, feel free to call your coach from time to time for advice. And perhaps at some point a new challenge will spur you to decide to hire them again. We see it often.

There are many accountability strategies. Some leaders may give themselves weekly grades on their performance. Others may ask accountability partners to do the same or provide bracing assessments of goals met and unmet. Others will habitually seek out stakeholders in their continued commitment to feedback. Still others will adopt a reflective questionnaire, which Marshall outlines in the next section.

Simply stated, we are not here to instruct. Our goal is to open eyes to the variety of options available. These pages have aimed to stimulate, not dictate. And when we move to part three, those who have read us thus far can elect to heed our wider vision or not, whether they be coachable leaders or coaches themselves.

A MOMENT WITH MARSHALL: OPEN TO ACCOUNTABILITY

For the past twenty-five years, I have had someone call me on the phone almost every day to listen to me do my Daily Questions. The questions keep me accountable because they force me to reflect on whether, that day, I have tried to do the things that are most important to me: things that are too easy to neglect.

At the moment, I have about fifty questions about subjects like my health, my work, my time, and my relationships. Because I am taking responsibility for these things, I begin the questions by saying, "Today, did I do my best to…?" The questions change over time. And if you do this, then your questions will be different from mine. But there are six I always ask. "Today, did I do my best to set clear goals?

To make progress toward goal achievement? To be happy? To find meaning? To build positive relationships? To be fully engaged?" If you ask those six questions every day, then you will experience greater satisfaction with life.

If I do my Daily Questions every day, I get better. If I don't do them, then I don't get better. I need to be held accountable. And I have the humility to know I am too cowardly and undisciplined to do that alone, which is why I have someone call me. None of us have that much willpower. Why do top tennis players have coaches? Why do people in good shape hire personal trainers? They admit they are not going to do it on their own.

Half the people I do Daily Questions with quit in two weeks. It is very difficult to look in a mirror and face the reality of our lives. It is especially hard when we have been fooling ourselves for the past forty-five years. It is so much easier to blame others. But when we start to take accountability, we start to take control over our lives. That's where the magic happens.

EXECUTIVE SUMMARY
The Accountability Factor

You've started the coaching journey to effect change. To ensure *lasting* change, even beyond the coaching engagement, you'll want to invest in accountability.

- **Be aware of backsliding.** Backsliding is inevitable after the coaching process is completed. This should not be a reason for despair. Rather, it is a call for ongoing accountability.

- **Marry accountability with feedback.** With feedback, you want to know what actions you should be taking. With accountability, you want to know how well you are performing those actions. Feedback and accountability can be uncomfortable, but your coach will help you become more comfortable with the process. As we've said before, "thank you" is always the best response to feedback or accountability.

- **Get help with accountability.** Accountability comes in many forms—via a coach, colleague, or friend—but the key is to make it external and not to rely wholly on internal drive and motivation. It is wise to recruit an accountability partner, a trusted person who can assess your progress.

- **Broadcast your commitment.** It does not suffice for leaders to simply be aware of their commitment to accountability. They should freely and frequently share their commitment with their colleagues. External perceptions of leaders are crucial, and a leader's outward accountability can help with that perception.

- **Analyze accountability calls.** Be mindful of who or what you hold yourself accountable to. Bad choices exist. Just like change, feedback, and action, accountability calls for a clear-eyed assessment of benefits and downsides.

Coaching doesn't end with the coaching engagement. Accountability—reporting to others—should trigger the virtuous cycle of change, feedback, action, and accountability, a cycle of growth that should guide leaders throughout their careers.

PART THREE

TO WHAT END?

We wrote this book because we are passionate about leaders getting the most value from coaching possible. In part one, we shared our experience so that you would be better able to understand the world of coaching, how it operates, and how you can approach it. We described the kind of leaders that can benefit from coaching and why coaching is different from other forms of support that are available. We scratched the surface of misconceptions about coaching. We described the process of coaching from search to selection to engagement, and we shared our approach to getting started.

In part two, we shared what we consider to be the four keys to becoming coachable: being open to change, feedback, action, and accountability. With these tools, the right coach, supportive accountability partners, and an invigorating organization, we truly believe you can do anything. The sky is the limit, and we've shown you how a coach can help you launch to new heights.

We could stop here. After all, you picked up this book to learn what coaching is and how you can get the maximum benefit from it. That's it. Right? But instead of calling it a day, we will now go on to pose the age-old question: *To what end?*

We have a different vision for your potential as a leader, one that extends and expands beyond the coaching engagement and even the business environment. If you are willing to indulge us a little longer, we would like to share our thoughts on the potential that you possess as a leader in all aspects of life. There is no obligation to stick with us here. But if you do, we look forward to highlighting how to go beyond your development as a leader within the confines of the office and how to propel yourself to the next level: becoming a better human who, like a pebble thrown into a pond, will inspire a ripple effect that will change the world.

In part three, we hold out an offering and an invitation. We're going to help you understand not just how you get more from coaching, but what you can do with what you have just learned. We're sharing this offering with you, wherever you are. If you're in a place to accept it, that's wonderful. If you're in a place to be able to take it one step further by routinely applying it to your life, that's also wonderful. And, by the way, if you're not in a place to meet it, that's okay, too.

The first chapter in this section, "Within You," imagines how you will show up post-coaching to have the highest impact for yourself and the people around you. The starting point is you. If you are like most leaders, you picked up this book and got this far because you want to be a better leader. You want to have a better career, and you want the people on your team to be more productive and feel like you are supporting them in their work. You understood that coaching would make you more effective, more valuable, and that you might even get a promotion. We call that Rising. Rising is about creating expansion by being a better leader, getting more from your teams, and being better able to manage up and down in your organization. If you accomplish Rising, you have a great deal to feel proud of. You have worked hard to reach this place of responsibility and influence.

That said, we would like to offer you more. We invite you to consider a mindset and behavior that we call Flourishing, a more aspirational and inspirational approach to life at large. We will describe how we understand the trajectory of becoming a leader and how you can transcend Rising to truly Flourish. We will give you examples of how Flourishing leaders show up and the breadth of their accomplishments.

It's no coincidence that the tools in the openness framework not only allow you to become coachable, but they are also the keys to being a better leader and human being. Great leaders and great people welcome change, accept feedback from others, take action, and embrace accountability. By adopting the framework, you're already one giant step closer to incorporating the principles of Flourishing in your life and leadership, both internal and external to the office. We hope to inspire you to act on the further potential that we believe you can unlock as a leader, human being, and contributor to the expansion of those around you.

In the final chapter, "With Us," we make the case that Flourishing is not a lone pursuit; instead, it happens in quiet collaboration with all of us. Not just us, the authors, but us, our collective society—every individual in our orbits.

CHAPTER EIGHT

WITHIN YOU

A NEW WAY OF BEING

Crack open a dictionary, and you will see a definition of *Flourishing* that speaks of developing rapidly and successfully thriving. Blooming and blossoming. However, we've attached a different meaning to the word, one that speaks to our aspirations for each of the leaders we work with and beyond.

Aristotle coined the term *eudaemonia*, which is usually translated as "the condition of living well." We've adopted a similar outlook and called it *Flourishing*. Aristotle stated that this type of living transcends and expands beyond superficial happiness and is "the way we are supposed to be as human beings."[25] Rising, the management ascent strategy that we'll explore in the next section, also places significance on expansion. However, Rising's version of expansion is focused on the growth of individual leaders, specifically their accomplishments, advancements, and successes.

Flourishing takes it one step further. When a leader is truly Flourishing, they're not only lifting themselves up—they're lifting everyone around them up as well. Like the notion of a tide lifting all the boats in a harbor, living a life with a Flourishing perspective allows the career you have and the life you live to be more influential and more far reaching than it could have been otherwise. When we're Flourishing, it's in many directions and in many dimensions. It's the difference between leaving behind a life or a legacy. Flourishing is expansive. And with expansive growth, we grow together.

We have already established that within the business environment, the ideal leader should be moving ever forward in a virtuous cycle. But what about that which lies beyond the business environment: in other words, everything and everyone else? From a coaching engagement, a leader acquires transferable skills. The behaviors acquired by those who have been successfully coached, such as listening with empathy and seeing feedback as a gift, can be applied to all endeavors, not just business. When one applies those lessons learned, one becomes a better leader, yes. But one also has the power to become a better spouse, parent, citizen, community member, and agent of change in the wider world. Leadership by example works everywhere. Flourishing spreads its benefits far and wide.

Flourishing is not merely aspirational; it is inspirational. By becoming a better leader and human being, you unlock the potential to create human Flourishing all around you. One of the advantages of having been successfully coached is that you undoubtedly have the tools to better your interactions—not only within the office, but external to it as well.

Interactions entail relationships. We said much earlier that coaching and business are human endeavors. The same holds true for all interactions in life—interactions with other people, the environment around us, and even within ourselves—these relationships constitute the firmament of growth. You are in a constant flow of exchanging feedback and perceptions all the time. When you learn how to engage with that process in a healthy way, you create a space for people to expand, change, and create real transformation. Upon reflecting on our past experience, most of us agree that both minor and major transformations happen as a result of being in relationships with others. That's certainly true in life, and it can be easier to point out those examples. It's also true in business, though many business leaders—those who are in the process of Rising as opposed to Flourishing—may not see it as clearly. That's understandable and to be expected.

What we have observed in working with hundreds of executives is that, at their core, the struggle is rooted in relationships. Interactions and relationships are a driving force in business, deeply intrinsic to the beating heart of any organization. One of a leader's chief priorities concerns relationships, in one form or another. Rarely do things happen outside of an interaction- and relationship-focused context, in life *and* in business. Leaders must make hard decisions—such is the nature of leadership. Sometimes leaders will need to cut partnerships short, let people go. These are often some of the most challenging situations that leaders face. Flourishing doesn't mean the absence of pain or challenges, but it does mean that leaders are armed with the tools to face them: a strong set of values, emotional courage, and respect for the humanity of others. We also posit the following: *No leader should go at it alone.*

The legend of leaders as lone riders spurring their mounts

through the chaparral has long ago been put out to pasture. Through coaching, you will have learned that leadership is a collective project. An amusing maxim of present-day leadership thinking from well-known thought leader John Maxwell is, "He who thinks he leads, but has no followers, is only taking a walk." We have said earlier that what others hear means more than what leaders say. To this we add that what leaders do—and the way in which that doing impacts others—means even more.

Embracing others is a prerequisite of the Flourishing model. Human Flourishing happens one relationship at a time, each person contributing their strengths and experiences to reinforce the growth of the other. It's a give and take that is cyclical, concurrent, and happening all around us, to one degree or another. Moment to moment, a rising tide is invisible to the eye. But leave the shore and come back a few hours later, and you'll be able to see the monumental shift that has happened across the coastline. The same is true of the way Flourishing relationships impact organizations, industries, families, and the world.

By adopting a Flourishing mindset, you will have the tools to consciously elevate the people around you, both in and out of the office. And you'll do that in large part due to the skills you've gleaned from coaching and can transfer to others.

Correctly coached, you are the pebble thrown into the pond, causing ripples to radiate. Simply put, we have noticed that people who transform themselves have the power to, in turn, transform others. Not a bad purpose in life, no? But for Flourishing to truly work its magic, the changes you envision must come from within you—and in the following section we aim to clarify the different approaches to growth that culminates, in our view, in Flourishing.

Our goal isn't to preach, but to share a perspective on work and life that has given back to us personally and to those around us time and time again. Those who think our goal is too heady may still want to poke their nose in the next few pages before deciding to close the book altogether, though we promise not to be offended if you do.

That said, we hope you join us. We already know you're doing great things and leaving a mark on the world. We can't wait to see how Flourishing will propel you even farther.

ON STRIVING, PEOPLE-PLEASING, RISING, AND FLOURISHING

To better understand what we believe to be the most powerful leadership mindset, we will examine all four different approaches to leadership: Striving, People-Pleasing, Rising, and Flourishing. The four do not form inescapable silos; a leader may switch management strategies at different stages of their career.

Given the amount of information we have imparted in this chapter, it is first useful to illustrate each of the leadership approaches from a high level.

What follows is a two-by-two grid. The x-axis (the horizontal) has two elements: "Me" on the left; "We" on the right. This refers to the leader's perspective as either self-centric or relationship/team-centric. The y-axis (the vertical) also has two labels: "extractive" on the bottom; "expansive" on the top. This refers to whether a leadership approach is extracting (subtracting) or expanding (adding) value to an organization. When we plug in our four approaches, this is the result:

On the bottom left, we see that Striving is rooted in a self-seeking effort to continuously achieve outcomes for themselves, prioritizing those over the journey or the fellow travelers on the journey. Strivers often do not understand how to enlist a valuable team and lead well, so they achieve little growth. Extraction of value from the organization is likely due to poor collaboration and reduced morale.

Bottom right, we see that while People-Pleasing involves a praiseworthy collective perspective, its inefficiencies and continual self-sacrifice can exact their toll and extract value certainly from the individual and often from the organization as well.

Top left, we see that Rising also has a self-centric perspective. But Risers know how to create value for their organizations. Their driving factor in creating that value is to ultimately move into positions of greater responsibility or authority.

Finally, at the top right, we see Flourishing. The Flourishing leader honors the collective health of the team and organization and can chart the path to expanding value for the organization while prioritizing both themselves and those in their orbit. It is expansive and generative in nature.

Now, let's expand upon each of these leadership approaches.

STRIVING

One common approach to leadership is what we call Striving. Striving refers to the act of making a strong, persistent effort to achieve a goal, fulfill a purpose, or overcome challenges. It involves dedication, hard work, and perseverance in pursuing objectives or ambitions. People may Strive for personal growth, career success, or a variety of other accomplishments in their lives. And this is not necessarily negative as its root driver is determination. It can become negative, however, when that determination is the only driving force, manifesting in unhealthy or even harmful ways.

For example, if someone is described as "always striving for more," we can interpret it as a positive trait, showcasing their ambition and drive. On the other hand, if unbridled reaching becomes more important than relishing the successes along the way, Striving can quickly become a toxic management style. If your team is constantly receiving the message that you are only focused on yourself and that what they are achieving is never enough, they may feel burned out or unfulfilled by their work. In short, we believe one of the negative hallmarks of Striving is a constant chasing in the service of self, where the reward is never sufficient.

In this approach, it is common to view climbing the ladder of responsibilities as a zero-sum game. I'm up. You're down. In

Striving, the focus is on what I'm doing, what I want, how I will ascend through the ranks. Whereas some other approaches have the collective "we" in mind, Striving is about "me."

While common in many corporate settings, the collateral damage of Striving is that it sometimes adds no value to the company; in fact, it may extract value through bruised colleagues, fallen productivity, and the usual perils of go-it-alone leadership. After uncovering this realization during a successful coaching engagement, Strivers often adopt our third leadership approach, Rising, if only because they want themselves and their company to prosper.

ON STRIVING

Striving, we maintain, is characterized by ineffectual exertion. Someone can expend a lot of energy but make little to no progress if they are focused on ill-serving goals. Striving is about personal advancement without enjoying the journey or fellow travelers. We've said it before, and we'll say it again: Collaboration is essential to maximizing growth and effecting change. With that in mind, you can see how Striving will not yield great results.

Striving can be summed up by the classic parable of the difference between the bricklayer who sees himself as one who lays bricks rather than the bricklayer who views himself as a church builder. The former cares about the confines of their role, the latter about what they are building.

For example, our friend Miguel was a classic Striver. He was working in the tech industry in a job that paid the bills but offered him little to nothing in terms of fulfillment. He knew from his first day at the company that his goal was to leave

ASAP. He was desperate for the opportunity to build and grow his own company, to create something himself. This drove him to try to found a number of start-ups with friends—he was like a moth to a flame when it came to any new business idea. The one that seemed the most viable was to start an electrolyte beverage company with a close friend. The two of them sourced materials, created a lot of test batches, and even set up booths on various running trails where they asked runners to try their beverage and provide feedback.

Miguel was driven relentlessly to make the business succeed. In his mind, this was his ticket out of corporate America. But anyone who starts or builds a business knows how challenging it is and how many hurdles one needs to clear. Sadly, a single-minded focus on the outcome is not enough. You must also savor the process, or else you cannot overcome all of the obstacles. This is what happened with Miguel; his business partner moved away, and he realized that he simply didn't care enough about the product to continue the work on his own. As the saying goes: "A man who loves walking will go farther than the man who loves the destination."

Miguel may not have put it in these terms at the time, but he was Striving. He was running from something rather than running toward it. Striving is a lot like the quote commonly attributed to Einstein as the definition of insanity: doing the same thing over and over and expecting a different result. It's hard for those caught in the cycle of Striving to break free.

Miguel realized that if things stayed as they were then he would continue spinning his wheels with no progress. He made the brave decision to seek help. He enlisted the help of a coach to support him in creating a meaningful life and career for himself.

With his coach's guidance, he began succeeding in his job while reducing his working hours. He was recognized for his contributions and given more and more authority. He found meaning in his work and in leading his team. He had successfully closed his Striving chapter.

But he knew that there was still more. His life had been transformed with the help of his coach, and he wanted others to experience the same. So, he decided to become a coach himself. As Miguel Flourished, so did his coaching clients. And that's how Flourishing works: It's contagious, and it starts with each of us.

But the Striving ethos is everywhere and very common. Traditionally speaking, sales roles have long had a reputation as being a place where people Strive; they Strive to be number one, they Strive to beat the competition, and they Strive to outperform each other. When Alec Baldwin's character in the iconic movie *Glengarry Glen Ross* declares that the top salesperson gets a Cadillac, the second gets steak knives, and the third gets fired, he establishes a pretty clear demarcation between winners and losers.

When we Strive for something, we are playing, as we have said earlier, a zero-sum game requiring winners and losers—everything comes at the cost of something or someone else.

As a career sales professional and leader, Andy found himself working in some environments fueled by a level of competitiveness that can be toxic. He remembers, very early in his career, a dispute about territorial boundaries between two salespeople that turned decidedly nasty, descending into two grown men taking swings at each other in the parking lot. No marked harm was done in the end, other than to their reputations; however, it highlighted the destructive nature of Striving over all else.

As Andy progressed in his career, he discovered that he was increasingly uncomfortable in the traditional sales culture and often felt out of place. He found himself wondering if it was possible to keep winning at every opportunity he could *and* do it in a way that creates benefit for all stakeholders.

As a result, he adopted a non-zero-sum approach wherever he could, getting creative about partnerships and staying agile with his approach. One of Andy's most rewarding experiences was receiving the following feedback from a prestigious client: "That was the most 'non-salesy' sales experience I've ever had."

When Andy moved away from the Striving mindset and instead prioritized the client's needs and wants as they related to the product he was selling, he found much greater success—and personal satisfaction with his career—than ever before. He was able to meet and exceed the original, two-dimensional Striving goals he had set for himself. His mindset shift created growth for both himself and his company, increasing his personal fulfillment as a result.

In sum: Strivers take more for their own benefit, ultimately extracting value from an organization.

PEOPLE-PLEASING

A second approach to leadership is People-Pleasing, in which the executive will do anything to be liked. Although humane and laudable in its prioritization of "we," it can be problematic. In the darkest scenario, the leader may even sacrifice their own needs or the overall needs of the organization to satisfy those of other individuals. In doing this, they may eventually burn out or lose the esteem of their colleagues. Constantly bending to the demands of others will be noticed—and perhaps exploited.

The urge to please people may arise from a variety of circumstances: conflict avoidance, habitual indecision, or perhaps something as innocuous as a sunny disposition. Some People-Pleasers may have been brought up this way, to be the dutiful daughter or the subservient son. One person we interviewed gave an entirely different motive: "I'll tell you from my own experience what People-Pleasing is," she said. "It is a desperate need to prove. That was my own experience in college and my first job. It is the desperate need for the approval of other people to prove to myself that I'm worth something."

Of course, doing the opposite and displeasing people to get ahead can backfire. Constantly ruffling feathers for no clear purpose can lead to team demoralization. What is certain, however, is that advocating for oneself and one's vision is a key trait of good leadership that commands respect from a team. Coaching will have taught leaders not to go overboard in their self-advocacy. A good coach encourages leaders to listen and learn before taking appropriate action. That is not at all the same as repeatedly bowing to others as a leadership tactic. People-Pleasers will, on multiple occasions, knowingly bypass the most fruitful solution in order to placate others. At best, they may be perceived as lacking executive direction; at worst, deep in the pockets of those with a vested interest in the outcome of certain actions. People-Pleasing will not work in the long run and often extracts value from a company in the short and long term. After all, you cannot pour from an empty cup.

ON PEOPLE-PLEASING

We can dress People-Pleasing up all kinds of ways to justify it to ourselves: "I'm just a giver." "I just like to see others happy." "I don't want to appear overly confident." Excuses are usually a respectable screen to mask what it really is: sacrificing oneself for the approval and happiness of others. Or, in other cases, an innate desire not to rock the boat.

Allow us to illustrate with an example that may be familiar to many. Joelle was working a corporate job, one in which she had been given a lot of responsibility, and she wondered if she was really good enough for the position. But rather than focus on the essential tasks she would need to master to thrive in the role, her subconscious took her in a different direction. Instead, her attention went to winning over the members of the twenty-person team by becoming the go-to person whenever someone needed help or had an idea.

Wanting other people to like us is a normative aspect of the human psyche. However, People-Pleasing is sinister and sneaks up on us quickly. Joelle cared so much about lending a sympathetic ear and helping hand that she sabotaged her own ability to get the job done effectively. Her agenda became the onslaught of needs and requests of others, not the tasks required to keep the business running. She had opened the floodgates and couldn't close them again. She didn't want to turn anyone away. When others thanked her for her support, she felt good about herself. She felt like she had succeeded at something; when others viewed her as valuable, she saw value in herself. But inside, she was drowning. She had to work late into the evenings to try to get her actual job done so that she could go about her preferred day job of People-Pleasing.

Here's where the cunning nature of People-Pleasing comes in: On paper, Joelle was receiving great feedback from her peers. But her boss knew that she wasn't completing core responsibilities on time or to the best of her ability, and that she could do better. And her wife certainly knew she could improve her self-care and mental health.

The way out for Joelle? Recognizing that the relationship that mattered most of all was her relationship with herself. She couldn't pour from an empty cup. The only sustainable solution would be to learn her own boundaries and respect them. Only through this could she learn and show respect for herself, and ultimately, give back to her organization and family in a productive, supportive, holistic way.

In sum: People-Pleasers give more for the benefit of others, often at the cost of themselves. Ultimately, this extracts value from an organization.

RISING

The third leadership approach represents the tradition of advancing in one's career by climbing the corporate ladder. Steeped in the hierarchical model, Rising is what we have inherited from the way work has always been done. Rising leaders pour themselves into the mold, shaping themselves in whatever way necessary to reach the next milestone of success. Rising through a company often results from a combination of efforts, including hard work, strong performance, commitment, leadership skills, and networking with the right people. These leaders stay within the bounds of the playing field to appeal to those

above them in order to receive promotions, move into positions of greater responsibility or authority, and gain increased
decision-making power.

A Rising leader is someone who knows what they need to do
to reach higher levels, and they organize themselves and others
to achieve it. The resulting steady-hand-at-the-tiller quality
expands value for a company, as the leader guides everyone to
know their place and perform their tasks in an orderly fashion.

Nonetheless, Rising shares a characteristic with Striving:
These leaders more than likely do not bring others with them
on the way up. They may Rise at the expense of the others, but
not necessarily so. However, at their core, these leaders place
the emphasis once again on "me," on their own climb to the
top of the mountain. While this type of leadership expands
value for the organization, the marked betterment of others
is a byproduct of circumstance rather than a result of intentional effort.

ON RISING

From an early age, Ali was an ambitious entrepreneur who knew
how to make money in almost any endeavor he embarked on.
A dean of his college enlisted a friend to mentor him during
his senior year and support his growth from solo entrepreneur
to leader. Ali's mentor reviewed his background and was duly
impressed by his thinking and accomplishments. Clearly this
young man was a natural salesman and marketer and, with
some guidance, had the potential to have a strong career in
that discipline. They set up a call, got to know one another, and
eventually became friends.

Ali was a classic Striver. He would describe himself as a lone wolf and loved to use expressions like "eat what you kill" to describe his approach to business. In fairness, Striving was working for him. He was making good money and working hard while maintaining his own schedule. He was extremely creative, and his ideas were a wonderful combination of exhilarating and value-creating. Clients loved him, and he generated a significant amount of repeat business. His struggle was that, as a Striver, his entire business focus was on himself and how he could extract more value. Since he was creating a ton of value, tangible and intangible, for clients, they were happy to pay top dollar to work with him. Unfortunately, the same could not be said for the people he employed, always on a part-time basis. He paid the least he could and used them up before they eventually moved on. He was unable to build a team.

But Ali harbored ambitions to be more than a lone ranger, so he and his mentor discussed the difference between extraction and expansion, between trying to get the most value today and creating the most value over time. They considered the value of building a team and incubating talent. He was very open to taking action but struggled mightily with being open to change and input, perhaps a common struggle for someone as obviously smart and creative as he was. He had hired some great young people who were willing to work for him, and he was excellent at giving direction. The business grew, and he was Rising, growing into the role of leader focusing not only on his own success, but also on the success of his business. The business doubled and then doubled again.

But there was a limit to its growth, and that limit was Ali's inability to be open to change and input. His mentor worked on creating space for the other members of the team to share ideas and bring their perspectives to the work, but they were still yearning for more, and Ali struggled to create space for them. He always resisted feedback, and often, he would aggressively push back in preservation of his own ideas. He continued to be financially successful, but even as he was Rising and the company was growing, the team was not feeling the same benefits. At the end of the day, he was alone.

The opportunity presented to Ali by his mentor was the potential for Flourishing, and he turned away. Had he taken it, he would have been able to continue to expand his company and reach his goals while enriching the lives of those around him. Instead, he was resisting input and certainly was unwilling to be held accountable for his actions. Soon, key members of his team took their skills and started their own businesses doing similar or adjacent work to Ali's. Unfortunately, his firm soon developed a reputation for being a bad place to work. A few key clients left for other suppliers whose teams could support them better. What had gotten him to a level of success—his determination and creativity—could not get him to the next level of leadership in which his ability to lead and inspire a team was critical to success. He had achieved a level of Rising that provided enough financial success for him to retire young. But his own unwillingness to remain open to others' opinions and supportive of their own ascents meant he could never attain the level of Flourishing that would have enabled him to create an enduring business, maintain satisfying relationships, and expand the business beyond his capacity.

In sum: Risers create more for their own benefit. While this leadership approach ultimately expands the value of a company, the self-centric nature of this leader hinders their growth long-term.

FLOURISHING

This brings us back to the fourth and final leadership approach that might as well be in a separate dimension from the other three. There is no doubt that Flourishing leadership generates value for a company. Flourishing organizations are characterized by engaged and satisfied employees, strong teamwork, unbounded innovation, high productivity, and overall organizational success. Employees feel a sense of belonging and purpose, and they're able to achieve their full potential in a supportive and nurturing environment. The Flourishing executive, confident in their skills of leading by example, will invite others to the table to weigh in on an unresolved business challenge. They will include all their major stakeholders in the discussion, regardless of how different their talents and points of view may be. Flourishing is exemplified by inviting people to self-manage and problem-solve in their own way. No longer do leaders act Moses-like, swooping down with the Ten Commandments; they are instead collaborators keen to solicit the contributions and perspectives of others.

Flourishing is about "we," not "me." We all Flourish together, and we can't reach this level of leadership as a lone individual climbing a hierarchical ladder. We said earlier that the qualities that serve as the foundation of Flourishing must first come from within, and we maintain that belief. But once you have made the transformation inside, it does not take long for the Flourishing to spread. You are the pebble thrown into the pond. We hope you take the time to marvel at the impact you have.

ON FLOURISHING

Hubert Joly is a classic example of a leader who experienced very positive change and ended up being a great role model for Flourishing. A graduate of HEC Paris and Sciences Po, two of the most renowned business schools in the world, Hubert began his career at a leading global management consulting firm, rising quickly through the ranks to become partner. He then held a series of leadership roles demonstrating his ability to outperform and lead companies to success, delighting investors. Hubert says that his experience at these prestigious institutions led him to believe that it was important to be the smartest person in the room. He thought the value he brought to the table was coming up with the right answer to the problem at hand. And that worked for him until he met his next challenge.

When he was the CEO of the Carlson Companies, Hubert decided to work with Marshall. He was very open to learning and saw this as a potential way to move from becoming effective to becoming even better.

After leaving Carlson, Hubert accepted the challenge of leading Best Buy as CEO. When he took over as CEO, there was not a single analyst that recommended the company's stocks as a "buy," which was a very bad sign. All advice was to reduce head count; fire employees to reduce costs.

When he received coaching at Carlson, Hubert liked all the positive feedback he received from his stakeholders in his 360. He was very smart and dedicated, exhibited the highest levels of integrity, and had a great knowledge of the business. But he initially struggled with the negative feedback. As his coach, Marshall helped him process the negative feedback and guided him to embrace asking for help. Hubert embraced this process. Eventually one of his favorite phrases became, "My name is Hubert, and I need help."

He recognized that setting the goalpost of being the smartest leader is overrated, and that creating the right environment for others to thrive is the key to successful leadership. Hubert recounts the story: "As leaders, we often tend to focus on the 'What' of an idea. But it's more interesting to focus on the 'Why' and the 'How.' And the 'How' of turning around Best Buy involved the opposite effect that *cut-cut-cut* would have had. We took a very human-centric approach, which started with listening to the front lines."

To support that effort, Hubert spent time working in a Best Buy store in St. Cloud, Minnesota. He asked the front-liners: "What's working? What's not working? What do you need?" His job was as simple as posing the question and taking notes. And eventually, Hubert did as he was told...by the employees. The people on the front lines had all the answers; all he had to do was listen.

It was also about reshaping the team at the top. As it relates to turning the ship around, head-count reduction was the last resort. Oh, and he learned a new word: *heartcounts*. To Hubert, heartcount reduction was even more of a last resort.

In Hubert's own words: "Leadership starts with figuring out who you are and who you want to be as a leader. At the end of the day, a business is a human organization, made up of individuals working together in pursuit of a goal. And that's what matters, as does the idea of thinking about the company as a purposeful human endeavor of innovation. It's the idea of pursuing that noble purpose, putting people at the center, embracing all stakeholders, and treating profit as an outcome. The idea of the leader as the superhero who knows everything and tells other people what to do—not so effective. Being clear about your purpose, your principles, and being driven by words that we never used to use in business, such as authenticity, humility, empathy, and humanity. These are very important words." Hubert Joly chronicles his journey in his bestselling book *The Heart of Business,* and today he teaches these lessons as a Harvard Business School professor who found success in his transformation to Flourishing.

In sum: Flourishing creates more for the benefit of all. This leader is invested in the success of their organization, their stakeholders, and themselves, while appreciating and channeling the impact they can have on the world.

RISING VERSUS FLOURISHING

If you've made it this far, you likely have an idea as to which leadership category you fall into. The revelation may have been uncomfortable or rewarding. Perhaps it wasn't a revelation at all, and it was instead a reassurance of who you are or who you hope to be. In truth, most good leaders we encounter pre-successful coaching fall squarely into the Rising category. We must emphasize: the majority of Rising leaders are smart, capable, caring individuals. But, they may not yet have realized their full potential, or their capacity for active, positive—as opposed to neutral or unknowingly negative—impact on those around them.

Soon after a coaching engagement begins (or perhaps, over the duration of reading this book), those leaders may begin to see how Flourishing truly raises all of us up. They may start to conceptualize what their own Flourishing looks like and create a plan to reach it. It is this moment that the true, unwavering power of successful executive coaching is fully realized. And to take it one step further: This moment is made all the more possible by the leader first *becoming coachable.*

With all of this in mind, we have crafted a table that provides a view into how the two expansive leadership approaches— Rising and Flourishing—compare. Neither approach is bad, but Flourishing, we maintain, is better.

RISING	FLOURISHING
me	we
zero sum	non-zero sum
competitive	collaborative
success first	relationship first
individualistic	collectivistic
fit the mold	seen for self
value grabbing	value creating
additive	exponential
hierarchical	democratic/egalitarian
centralized	distributed
reward/ego-driven	purpose-driven
mechanistic	humanistic
rigid	adaptable and expansive
imposed, external fairness	every unique human gets what they need
"here's what we need from you"	"what do you want to contribute?"
somewhat generative	guaranteed generative

We now turn to the road that leads to Flourishing. Not only can it be paved by the lessons learned in a coaching engagement, but it can also reveal itself, almost unsuspectedly, through decisions you make in the heat of a moment. We call those moments forks in the road.

FORKS IN THE ROAD

When one is ascending in leadership, the road ahead is paramount. Challenges come at you from many directions, forcing you to work hard to hold on to your right-of-way. In the headlong journey of your career, it is often difficult to know whether you are Striving, People-Pleasing, Rising, or Flourishing. That is understandable; the pressure to move forward, to slay the newest dragon, does not invite introspection.

Yet you may occasionally look in the rearview mirror and see something in retrospect that you did not see at the time. Something in that moment sparked you to change, forced you to decide, prompted you to act in one way and not another. Something caused you to switch silos in your approach to leadership. That moment was a fork in the road. Back then, in the rush of events, you probably did not ask yourself, "Am I serving other people? Or just myself?" But in deciding on the way to go, you may have *taken into consideration* the concerns of others. And this may have led you to take the first steps from "me" to "we," from prioritizing ego to prioritizing team.

We now turn to describing three such forks in the road, each with a different path chosen.

When Alan Mulally left his job as the head of Boeing to take over as CEO of Ford Motor Company in 2006, he knew there would be challenges. The automaker was expected to lose $17 billion that year. Leadership was struggling to face the problems, and there was no way to hide them. The company was at a fork in the road and needed to start working together. Here is the story as told by Alan.

When he first arrived at Ford, he noticed that every day in the *Detroit News*, there was an article by journalist Bryce Hoffman. The stories were horrible accounts about Ford's production issues, labor relations or harassment, or quality concerns. Alan noticed that each article described the details clearly. So he took one of the articles to his leadership team, and he asked if they had seen the articles and if the information was true. The leadership team responded affirmatively on both counts.

Alan understood there was a lot to address at Ford, given the huge amount of money they were planning to lose that year. But what interested him most was that the only way for the journalist to get that information was if the employees were calling the press and sharing the stories. Alan again asked his leadership team for suggestions about how to address this issue of the leaks. One of the leaders recommended identifying the employees who were going to the press and making a public spectacle of them. This leader reasoned that this would be an example to the others, and the stories would stop.

Alan immediately rejected this suggestion. Instead, he called the journalist, Bryce, and asked how he was getting such accurate stories. Alan appealed to the Detroit journalist's love for Ford, saying, "We don't know each other, but you know why

I'm here. There's only one reason: to help save this organization and create a viable, profitable, growing company for the good of all stakeholders and for the greater good. So, please trust me, because I need to understand what's going on."

Bryce told him that he simply listened to the messages on his answering machine each morning and night; all the stories were there. Each caller would leave a detailed message along with their name and telephone number and an invitation to please call if he needed any information or clarification. Bryce reminded Alan that the Ford employees knew that the company was set to lose $17 billion. They knew all the issues existed. And they thought that the leadership of the company didn't know about it. Because if they knew about it, they would have done something about it. Families that had worked at Ford for multiple generations were watching the company go under, and the leaders weren't addressing the issues. So their last resort was to call Bryce and tell their stories, hoping they would be heard.

Alan already knew that to turn the company around, they would need to engage all of their employees to be part of the solution. This situation motivated him to address the issues and start a free flow of information throughout the company. Alan set an example from the top of the company, and he made it his mission to solicit candid employee feedback and insight. He made it known that sharing information about company problems was welcome and even applauded by upper management. The issues became visible, and employees could see that they were being addressed. Employee sentiment began to shift. For the first time in a long time, they had some hope.

After two months, all the negative articles ceased, and Bryce began writing more about the turnaround. Curious to know what happened, Alan called Bryce and asked, "Why are there no more articles about the problems at Ford?" to which Bryce replied, "Alan, there are no more messages on my answering machine."

Alan recounts that time: "Think about it. Every week that data flows up and down the organization. Everybody knew the issues. The frontline employees all knew first. But the leaders didn't know because they didn't want to hear it. But with our new open feedback policy, they knew everything. They were forced to see the issues, and the company was better for it. Known problems are gems for which you can say thank you. Once everyone knows what you're facing, you can deal with the problems together." And in overcoming issues together, the company and the employees and all of the stakeholders could prosper. And that's exactly what they did.

THE SOAP

Anita, an executive at a multinational consumer goods company, had a problem. Reports kept coming back to her that their personal hygiene products—namely, bars of soap—were not selling in certain regions of the developing world. The small kiosks in rural Africa carried Coca-Cola and potato chips, but not their soap. Not only was this a problem for her organization, but it had global health ramifications: Soap is fundamental for hygiene and public health; it is a building block of well-being for the world's poorest people. Yet, Anita's product consistently failed to go what is called "the final mile" in the business of distribution. Their soap was showing up in the cities but not in the countryside.

So, the executive canvassed her employees in these countries. "Find out what is causing the logjam," she requested of them.

Almost immediately, she received an answer. Kiosk operators in sub-Saharan Africa, for example, reported that they carried only what they could sell. They knew their clientele could simply not afford the family-size bars on offer. So Anita convinced their manufacturing division to downsize the soap, so that consumers could purchase it without straining certain budgets. The effect of the change soon revealed itself: Sales for her company rose, and people obtained the salutary substance that is soap. A win-win.

She had learned the value of seeing the problem from the consumer's point of view. Anita recognized that this concept had life-changing potential, and she knew she had a decision to make. She could continue her work within the company, moving up the corporate ladder and gaining increased responsibility but moving farther away from problems that made a tangible difference in people's lives. Or, she could take a risk and try to do similar things in the wider world, outside the walled enclosure of her organization. Rather than rise through the ranks, Anita chose to accept the risk of striking out on her own with the aim of Flourishing. She founded a group advocating for responsible corporate citizenship. Today, Anita and her team advise global brands to be more mindful of their consumers and to meet them wherever they are. Her social influence continues to grow, all because of a fork in the road disguised as a bar of soap.

THE REFLECTION

Less than a decade ago, coauthor Jacquelyn was a high-potential management prospect in an oil-and-gas company based in Texas. She was well-mentored, well-liked, and well on her way upward.

Yet there were a few jarring notes in her sweet song of success.

She felt internally unsettled when her work entailed maximizing profits over everything else. Was this really the way to make the world a better place? In one instance, the company had too much of a highly refined product on hand and nowhere to put or sell it. The sales team decided that the best business decision was to sell it at bottom dollar for use in dirty power generation in Africa, and that is what she was instructed to help facilitate: "It is better to burn it than to flood the market."

Other issues nagged at Jacquelyn. She had seen several rounds of layoffs in the industry in which company veterans with decades of loyalty and experience were let go when market conditions changed. She realized that what the industry called sustainability might have been more accurately described as compliance, doing the minimum to stay within the law and regulations. Sustainability projects were only undertaken if they would cut costs or grow profits in the short term. After all, the company had profits to prioritize and shareholders to keep happy.

Her fork in the road came in the form of a dream. In this dream, she was thirty years older, now firmly ensconced in the corner office. She looked around at the wood paneling when she caught her reflection in the window. She recognized her middle-aged self, now a seasoned professional who had reached her goals. But she could tell she no longer had that sparkle in her eyes. She looked older, not wiser. At the pinnacle of her career and yet defeated. She could feel she was weary of internal battles she had too often lost; she had compromised values along the way as she did what was necessary to gain the authority to create real change. But she knew she no longer cared about the things that had set her out on the journey in the first place. Rising had taken a fatal toll on her values. And she realized then that was too high a price to pay.

Within weeks, she left her job and joined 100 Coaches. She later discovered a poem written in 1934 by Dale Wimbrow, originally entitled, "The Guy in the Glass," that captures her experience:

When you get what you want in your struggle for self,
And the world makes you King for a day,
Then go to the mirror and look at yourself,
And see what that guy has to say.

For it isn't your Father, or Mother, or Wife,
Who judgement upon you must pass.
The feller whose verdict counts most in your life
Is the guy staring back from the glass.

He's the feller to please, never mind all the rest,
For he's with you clear up to the end,
And you've passed your most dangerous, difficult test
If the guy in the glass is your friend.

You may be like Jack Horner and "chisel" a plum,
And think you're a wonderful guy,
But the man in the glass says you're only a bum
If you can't look him straight in the eye.

You can fool the whole world down the pathway of years,
And get pats on the back as you pass,
But your final reward will be heartaches and tears
If you've cheated the guy in the glass.

Her fork in the road was more than a new direction; it was a *shift in perspective.* This is an opportunity for expansive growth and the adoption of Flourishing. At this type of pivotal moment, the leader sees beyond themselves and even their employees, and they can begin to see the effect that their business decisions have on the greater world.

In the final chapter, we discuss the ramifications of Flourishing to further flesh out what we are advocating. In fact, we are addressing not just you in the singular, but you in the plural. All readers. Constrained as we are by Standard American English, we cannot employ the South's "y'all," or Pittsburgh's "yinz," or Ireland's "ye." But you (and you and you) know what we mean.

EXECUTIVE SUMMARY
The Four Leadership Approaches

A leader acquires transferable skills from a successful coaching engagement and can apply the behaviors they acquire to all endeavors, not just business. In turn, one can become not only a better leader but a better spouse, parent, citizen, community member, and agent of change in the wider world. Flourishing, the most impactful form of leadership, includes the notion of expanding an organization's value combined with the aspiration to lift others in one's orbit, similar to lifting all boats with a rising tide. When we're Flourishing, it's in many directions and in many dimensions.

Becoming Coachable identifies four leadership approaches: Striving, People-Pleasing, Rising, and Flourishing.

- **Strivers** are focused on their own benefit, which ultimately extracts value. Striving is focused on a climb to the top involving a zero-sum game.
- **People-Pleasers** give more for the benefit of others (often at the cost of themselves), ultimately extracting value. People-Pleasing can be pernicious, whereby a leader sacrifices their interests for those of others.
- **Risers** create more for their own benefit, though a byproduct of their efforts creates more value for their organization. Rising, the traditional way of ascending the corporate hierarchy, is praiseworthy and honorable. But it can involve leaving others behind, all in the service of helping the leader's climb.
- **Flourishers** create more for the benefit of all, including for themselves, their peers, their company, and their world. Flourishing encompasses everyone in an organization; indeed, everyone in a leader's life. Sharing, openness, and compassion are its hallmarks.

Forks in the road are moments when leaders make decisions about which direction to take. They often happen in the heat of the moment and are generally analyzed in retrospect. At each fork, you can examine which leadership approach you are embracing at the time and decide if it is the one that will serve you, and those around you, the best.

CHAPTER NINE

WITH US

A CONVERSATION WITH SCOTT, JACQUELYN, MARSHALL, AND YOU

In the latter stages of writing this book, we decided to sit down and engage in a free-ranging conversation about coaching and Flourishing. This is an unconventional format for a book, we know. But we found the most invigorating aspects of book development were the insightful and energetic conversations we had with each other. They quickly became a favorite for us, and we found ourselves yearning for our readers to be present. Never one (or really, never three) to cave to a roadblock, we added one directly into the text. In it, we tell stories, tie up loose ends, and expand on other facets of leadership.

We invite you to take part in this ongoing conversation. At the conclusion of this chapter, we have provided a link for you to share your thoughts and experiences. We welcome them. Consider this digital platform an example of Flourishing, on which we hope many will contribute to the common good.

The conversation, which took place over one long spring day in New York, has been edited for concision and clarity.

THE MORNING

SCOTT: The idea that sparked the 100 Coaches Community came from a workshop Marshall attended called "Design the Life You Love," led by Ayse Birsel. In that workshop, he discovered he wanted to be like his heroes, Peter Drucker and Frances Hesselbein, and make it his life's work to teach people everything he knew.

I also attended Ayse's workshop and had a similar revelation. But my hero wasn't a world-class management thinker; my hero was someone closer to home: my maternal grandfather, Lou Konspore. I was very close to him until he passed away when I was ten. I always wanted to emulate him in my life, although I couldn't have realized what that meant until I heard this story:

My grandfather came to Connecticut from Russia in 1916 as a twelve-year-old boy along with his grandmother, mother, brother, and sister. His mother remarried, and he soon moved out of the house and got whatever jobs he could find until he assembled enough money to open his own stationery store, which later became a haberdashery, carrying all sorts of men's accessories. When the highway came through town, his store was taken away through eminent domain. Undaunted, he opened a new retail location on Summer Street in Stamford. It was a men's clothing store simply called Lou Konspore.

When I was a young boy, I would visit him in his store. I watched how he treated each person who walked in with great respect and love, whether or not they bought from him. He used to tell me how much he loved his work. He was passionate about fitting men with a suit that gave them confidence and respect and elevated their status in the eyes of others, and most importantly, in their own eyes. People entered the store excited to see him and left the store excited about themselves.

His mother's second husband was a man who tutored rabbis and students in Torah study. One student was a young man named Joe from White Plains. Eventually, Joe became a rabbi and got a job with the Orthodox community in Stamford. One day, my grandfather visited his mother's house and met Joe. He learned that Joe had received a prestigious new appointment. But then, with his experienced eye, he discreetly observed Joe's shabby suit, so he asked him what he intended to wear in his new role. Of course, the young rabbi did not have extra money to spare on a suit, so he said that he would lead the congregation dressed in the one suit that he had. Without missing a beat, my grandfather whisked him off to the store and made sure that he had clothing that celebrated his stature and suited (pun intended) the role he was about to undertake. He did not charge him for the suit. My grandfather saw his role as elevating people to do their best work, which was an ordained calling.

That story was typical of my grandfather. He was beloved by his customers because he loved them. He elevated them, and they elevated him right back. He never cared to be wealthy, yet he was one of the richest people I ever knew, never in need of anything, always willing to help. He was the fire chief in the local volunteer fire department and was very proud of the gleaming white fire engines they bought and housed at the firehouse. He was my hero because he was an example of what it meant to Flourish. He is my inspiration for this book.

But the story does not end there. Rabbi Joe, as he was fondly called, went on to have an illustrious career. I traveled with him to Israel for one of the most inspiring trips of my life. His sermons during the High Holidays were legendary, passionate, challenging, and elevating. He was an expansive thinker. Joe's obituary that appeared in the *Stamford Advocate* said it best: "His many accomplishments include meeting with Pope John Paul II eight times in his ongoing work to bring Jews and Catholics closer together and initiating a peace pilgrimage to Cairo and Jerusalem at the invitation of Egypt's President Anwar Sadat in 1978. He was appointed as representative to the United Nations nongovernmental organization representing the Synagogue Council of America in 1985 and cofounded the Center for Christian-Jewish Understanding at Sacred Heart University in 1993 to promote human rights." In other words: He excelled at his work, yes—but the heartbeat of his work was more than a list of accomplishments. It was the imprint he left on the lives of so many others. Myself included.

Flourishing is how we elevate the people around us, so they can elevate the people around them. We are unaware of which suit will make someone's day and which will be the first day in a journey of great importance. And when we embrace Flourishing as our model, every interaction becomes an opportunity for the kind of growth that we *all* need.

JACQUELYN: I love that story, and I know how it guides you and your actions. When we are Flourishing, we don't know when and with whom we will have the biggest impact, and it doesn't really matter. We are treating each person as though they might be the one who makes the most positive difference in the world. It sounds like your grandfather and Rabbi Joe did that daily. What a generous and expansive way to be!

Since we're talking about the wisdom of elders, I'd like to give you a story of my own. While we were on vacation, my husband and I met an elderly couple in their mid-nineties, named Charlie and Loretta.

We planned to have lunch with them, but Charlie had an unexpected (but not serious) medical issue come up and needed to go to urgent care. We offered to drive them, and since it was a Saturday afternoon we had the luxury of spending many hours together in the waiting room. We ended up having a wonderful, deep conversation about what makes a life meaningful and forged a beautiful connection with this older couple.

After we had gotten to know them, Charlie shared something that had been on his mind: "I've been thinking a lot about this. What do we get to take with us past this life? There's one thing, and one thing only, and that's our relationships. Our relationships last far beyond this lifetime. We're actually in relationships eternally." We fell silent as he said, "My goal in the final years of my life is to focus on being rich in relationships."

It was really beautiful. It was definitely a game-changing moment for me—to have that reflection from someone toward the end of their journey and to be able to insert that into my life in my twenties.

SCOTT: That story rings so true for you as someone who really prizes relationships. I love his insight that relationships last beyond our years, and I would add they last beyond our moments. We each remember and credit so many important people who live on in our memories and inform our actions. And we hope to have had a positive influence on others during our journeys. I can imagine the work you did with refugees in Greece certainly lasts in the memories of the people you met and helped there. How powerful it is to consider that there are many past versions of you living eternally in the minds of others.

The "lasting value of relationships" insight transcends time and space. That is why Flourishing is such an important idea—because these relationships are the substance of our lives. That's my grandfather's story, too. He lived his life through relationships. Think of what we've discussed previously. The three of us agree that the major transformations in our lives happened as a result of being in relationships with others. I think that it is rare for major shifts to happen outside of that context.

Marshall, when you think of people who Flourish, who do you think of?

MARSHALL: Of course the first person who comes to mind for me is my mentor and dear friend, Frances Hesselbein, who recently passed away at the age of 107. What a life of Flourishing that woman had. She was one of the most important leaders of all time, and Peter Drucker famously called her the greatest CEO in America. She was an extraordinary woman who led the growth and expansion of the Girl Scouts during her tenure as CEO by bringing a diversity of people and ideas to that organization, having a massive impact on generations of women. She was the first female CEO on the cover of *BusinessWeek*. She became the face of leadership development at West Point when she was ninety and was so beloved that the secretary of defense spoke at her remembrance of life service. It is hard to imagine many people who have had a more positive impact on more people than Frances.

Frances was one of the most powerful people you could have ever met. I don't think there was anyone that she was unable to stand eye to eye with. Though short in height, she was towering in stature and personal presence. And at the same time, she was remarkably humble. One of my favorite Frances stories goes as follows. One time, she asked me to speak at one of her meetings and, of course, I immediately agreed. Saying no to Frances was not an option. But I asked her, somewhat sheepishly, if it would be possible for someone to do my laundry while I was speaking. You see, I was traveling quite a bit and rather than stopping for the weekend to do laundry and repack, I could come to her conference. Of course, she said that would be no problem. I was set to speak and then I noticed Frances carrying my laundry right in front of the audience of her executives. That was pure Frances, making a point that no task was beneath her and setting that example to her leaders that no task should be beneath them. Frances led by example.

What I learned from Frances's life, what we can all learn from the example she set, is that our lives are made rich by what we give, not by what we receive. There was no one more generous and giving than Frances. And she was never without people around her, people who loved, admired, respected, and were inspired by her. Hers was truly a life of Flourishing and a demonstration of how one person, by putting everyone else first, elevates their own life and fills it with the riches that only relationships can bring. As Jacquelyn just shared in her story, relationships may be the only thing we can take with us after we are gone. Relationships are how the memories of us will survive. And by that standard, too, Frances continues to have a full and rich life.

JACQUELYN: Marshall, I love hearing your stories about Frances. Through the stories you and other 100 Coaches friends tell me, it feels like I knew her, and her life of Flourishing certainly inspires me. We are honored that she was a member, and we as a community are continuing her legacy.

During a team off-site, one of our key realizations was that everything we do is about relationships. By its very nature, coaching unlocks the transformative power of relationships. And we really are in a community with all our different coaches. That is the backbone of everything that we're doing.

And we're also in relationship with our clients. Cultivating strong, genuine relationships with them is a priority for us. Our insight tells us that it's not about efficiency. We've learned that creativity beats productivity every time, and it was this realization that produced outsize results. We said: Let's invest more resources. Let's spend more time together. Let's not try to maximize our efficiency or time; instead, let's try to actually maximize the relationship and the transformation. And I think that that has created real Flourishing for everyone. Business exists for people, not people for business.

SCOTT: That's where becoming coachable comes in. By becoming coachable, you, in turn, impact the lives of many down the road. And you can deepen your relationships. When you become coachable, you move from being static to fluid. You're able to do things you couldn't do before. You become more flexible, more open. And as you are now in this more open space, you can have relationships with all kinds of different people. That has been my experience, and what I have observed in the hundreds of people we have engaged with. I am astonished by the immense capacity for growth people have. And we recognize it is simple to understand on paper, but hard to practice in actuality. Methods we spoke about in part two can open people up for expansion they never imagined.

The whole relationship between you and yourself, you and the people in your organization, you as a human organism in the world...once you become coachable, things shift. This book's ambition is to simply help people open up a little bit, so that they can create a little change, which ultimately becomes a big change. This is like Buckminster Fuller's concept of the trimtab, which is a small strip of metal attached to a ship's rudder that helps initiate the turn of a big ship.

In some areas, we have to unlearn old habits of the mind. Getting to the top might not be the most satisfactory outcome. For his book, *The Dynamic Path: Access the Secrets of Champions to Achieve Greatness Through Mental Toughness, Inspired Leadership and Personal Transformation*, management thinker James Citrin interviewed dozens of top leaders who had reached the pinnacle of their careers. Many of them get there, look at the prize, and realize it's not the pinnacle that matters. Instead, creating more value in the world is really the ultimate achievement. We hear this time and again from leaders as they reach what they thought would be the peak of their career.

JACQUELYN: It is amazing how much "accepted wisdom" is not wise after all. We have so much to unlearn, including some accepted wisdom we learned in business school. Our friend and coach, Dr. Bonita Thompson, talks about how a balance sheet lists employees as expenses. Companies always say "our people are our greatest asset," but really they view them as expenses.

Expense also means expendable. But in this day and age, we can't view people that way. So many people, more than ever before, are information workers. Eventually, we'll probably be doing more work of the heart, not just work of the mind, even as AI and other technologies interface with humans. But that's another conversation.

The point is, when people are information workers, they're adding a ton of value that's not interchangeable. And they take years of experience and knowledge away with them when they leave the company. That's all of great value. And we already know that the time and money it takes to find and hire and train a new person is incredibly costly. So why do we treat our teams like expenses rather than as assets, which is what they really are?

SCOTT: Thinking of employees as assets makes a whole lot more sense, and, as you mentioned, is also consistent with how leaders talk and feel about employees who are making positive contributions. If you think of your people as an asset, when you give them training, it causes growth; you're improving your asset. If you get them coaching, you're improving your asset even more. And if you retain them, you're getting more longevity out of your assets.

If rather than four years we can get five years of useful life out of a machine, which is considered an asset on the balance sheet, then we've amortized the investment. That's a good thing. However, organizations are incentivized to reduce or get rid of expenses as quickly as possible. And unlike machines that often deteriorate with age, most employees continue to improve how they do their work, to deepen relationships, and to thicken the culture and community of the enterprise.

Practically, it works out beautifully because we don't have to change anything other than our mindsets. When you start thinking of the people that you're working with as your greatest assets—literally instead of figuratively—and you treat them as such, it actually starts to make sense. Retention becomes an act of growing your assets and is one of the most important things you do. And that creates Flourishing.

THE AFTERNOON

JACQUELYN: You said over lunch that you wanted to include a clear example of Flourishing leadership. Recently we spoke to Todd, founder and CEO of a Microsoft-certified training company. His company had around 150 employees when the 2009 financial crisis started to happen, and people were investing a lot less in training. At one point, their company was kind of on the verge of going under. They had to decide what expenses to cut. Again, are employees expenses, or are they assets?

So Todd gathers the entire company together, stands up in front of them, and says, "Companies can either be a roller coaster or a merry-go-round."

He goes on: "Listen, merry-go-rounds are fine. You know where you are, you know exactly where you're going, and you're just going in circles. It's very safe. And that's fine. Some people like that."

"But," he says, "this company is going to be a little bit more of a roller coaster. We're really building something here. And we really believe in what we're doing. But we've fallen on hard times. I'd like to let you know that you're welcome to leave; we'll pay severance for anyone who prefers to be on the merry-go-round. If you decide to stay on the roller coaster, it might be a little scary at moments. Like right now. We're going to cut everyone's pay by 25 percent for the next few months until we weather the storm, so that we don't have to fire anyone." He then asks them to let him know their decisions by the end of the week.

Only one person left the company. The rest of the employees stayed and took the 25 percent pay cut for six months until they came out on the other side. That initiative, his very real commitment to his employees, completely transformed the company's culture. I think it's just a beautiful story.

Todd was focused on Flourishing. This amazing leader came to us with a request. He told us that he wanted coaching to help him figure out what's next. He wanted to think more expansively as he grew his company to 250 people. "But," he said, "I don't know what I don't know yet. How can I go even further?"

Even a Flourishing leader can go farther with coaching. There's no upward limit to Flourishing. We can't wait to see where Todd's journey takes him.

MARSHALL: I tell a story of Flourishing in my last book, *The Earned Life*. It's the story of Mark Tercek who was a partner at Goldman Sachs, still in his forties. He was the perfect fit at Goldman—smart, charismatic, and exceptional at putting money to work for the firm. In his personal life, he was quieter and humbler, focused on his health, and a committed environmentalist. In 2005, he led the firm's environmental markets group. Three years later, an executive search firm asked him to recommend someone for the role of CEO at the Nature Conservancy. As he thought about possible candidates, his own name kept coming to mind. He certainly had the qualifications and the passion. In his heart, he really wanted the role, and his wife, Amy, also committed to the environmental cause, supported the move.

And yet, something blocked him from throwing his name into the hat. It would mean ending his financial services career at Goldman Sachs and moving from New York to Washington, D.C., to begin a new career in the nonprofit world. Mark and I went on a walk, and it was clear to both of us that this was something he really wanted for himself, because he felt he could make a meaningful difference in the world of environmentalism. And yet he hesitated and struggled to say yes. What was holding him back was the fear of what others would think of him if he left his prestigious job at Goldman for the job at the Nature Conservancy. I turned him around and looked him in the face and said, *"Come on, Mark! When are you going to start living your own life?"*

That was the jolt he needed. He called the recruiter, asked to be considered for the role, and was selected. He was allowing his Goldman definition of success from financial measures to obscure what he knew would be Flourishing for him. His tenure at the Nature Conservancy was a big success, and he was able to accomplish a great deal and have a life of personal satisfaction and environmental contribution.

SCOTT: Marshall, Mark's story is all too common. It is almost as though the world conspires to distract us from the work that allows us to feel truly fulfilled. Sometimes people are drawn by the feeling of being indispensable ("The organization needs me"). Other times, we feel we are on a winning streak and cannot leave until it's over ("Just one more big deal"). And then there is the time we feel stuck with no place to go. Once Mark let go of the fear of what others might think and embraced the idea of what he wanted, then he established a readiness for Flourishing.

Personally, I have never been clearer on the direction I'm going in and never been less attached to getting there. What's real to me about Flourishing is that it isn't about the end product; it is a way of being.

Let's say you go from Striving to Flourishing. Striving is all about the end product. It's not about the journey and not about being in a certain way. Flourishing is just the opposite. It is all about how you show up in each moment. It's all about the *being*— the way you are living your life in a way that is authentic to you.

One approach to Flourishing is to imagine the impact that you're going to have, the ripple effect. But another could just be: Embracing that you don't know. Echoing the case made in *The Earned Life*, we should let go of the effect that we might have in the future. There are too many factors that we don't control. Focus on the work you are doing now, which you do control. Understand what you are doing and why you are doing it, preferably in a context of the broad reverberations, not on the impact to you alone.

This creates Flourishing. And it doesn't matter where that Flourishing happens. Sure, you'd love it to happen for your family, and they may have the biggest impact on the world, but maybe not. It may be that the work that you do touches someone that you never meet, and that person does something spectacular because of it. Or it may be that all the work you do for Flourishing comes to naught. But that's not what's important. What's important is that you have switched your intention from figuring out how to aggregate the most for yourself to cultivating growth in general.

JACQUELYN: I have a probably bizarre analogy for what you've been talking about, but hear me out. Why do some people get the flu and others don't? You can have the flu, and no one else in your house gets sick. But then you go out grocery shopping, and someone in the grocery store gets sick because of you. It's whoever's receptive to the virus. Flourishing is like a positive pandemic. Whoever is susceptible to the contagion at that moment in time understands the power of Flourishing. And it's funny, sometimes those can be people who are very close to you, and sometimes they can be people that are somewhat external to your orbit. But for whatever reason, there's a time when they're really open. And the stars just aligned so that they get that thing that they needed at the moment they needed it—from you.

SCOTT: Another analogy is this: Flourishing isn't a flower growing. It is a field of flowers. You can't imagine a flower saying, "I want to own this field, and I'm going to be the only flower in the field." No, there are more flowers, more roots, in the field. And the more thriving flowers there are, the more pollinators that are attracted to the field. And on and on. This is what more life, more Flourishing, looks like.

MARSHALL: When I think of people who are Flourishing today, I have to think of Mike Sursock. Mike is one of the best operators in business and has consistently delivered exceptional results while caring passionately about people. He brought in some of the best advisors in the world and built a heartfelt and compassionate operations advisory from within one of the world's most successful private equity firms. Influenced by his leadership, the firm outperformed by financial measures and outpaced even more by human standards.

One day he and I were talking, and he showed me his Wheel of Life chart. He had developed this chart over the years based on the ethos of "life is now." He recognized that we only have one life, and to that end it is important to have everything deeply integrated including health, mindset, energy, family, community, and work. But equally important is that each of us find our own balance, which involves ranking each of these categories in order of meaning to us. Mike's chart provided clarity on his priorities and how much time and attention he was spending on them. Upon reflection, he realized that one important thing to him was spending time with his aging mother, who lived five thousand miles away. He realized there might only be a few years to give back to her.

That reflection opened the door to considering his other priorities and he quickly realized that he was trading career success for some of the more important and fulfilling parts of his life. He didn't need any more work success. He had accomplished what he had set out to accomplish. He had no need for any higher levels of prestige and accomplishment. When I asked him the age at which he expects to start slowing down and be physically unable to do everything he wants. He thought about it and replied, "Maybe ten to fifteen years." We realized that if he was planning to retire halfway through that time, he would have less than ten years of fully functional health and mobility.

It was one of those conversations that created change in

an instant. Mike realized that, given his stated priorities, he needed to make a radical change. He committed to spending more time with his mother, his grown children, and his wife. Mike shared his philosophy with his company, and they were supportive and understanding, allowing him to reduce his day-to-day responsibilities and significantly rebalance his priorities in his Wheel of Life. Mike was beaming when I saw him next. He is now living on his terms, not anyone else's. And he helps others do the same.

SCOTT: The realizations are endless. It's unbelievable what we don't see, even if it's staring us in the face, until someone helps us to see.

JACQUELYN: Exactly. That's how I felt when I truly understood the unlimited power of Flourishing for the first time. You can add two numbers together, perhaps even multiply two numbers together. But Flourishing is not addition or even multiplication. It's exponential. It's coming together. There are no turf wars and attitudes that say there's not enough for me. Flourishing is a world of abundance that says there is unlimited untapped potential and expansion available to us all. And by coming together, we start to see a ripple effect bigger than anything that any of us could experience on our own.

SCOTT: You have joined us on a journey of discovery, learning, and transformation. You have explored the foundations of coaching, the qualities of coachability, and the benefits of becoming coachable for yourself and others. You have seen how coachability can enhance your leadership, your life, and your contribution to human Flourishing. You have been offered a choice to embrace change, feedback, action, and accountability as a way of growing and improving. You have been challenged to become a better leader and a better person. You have been invited to join a community of like-minded people who share your vision and values. We hope you accept this invitation and continue to pursue your potential. We believe that when we work together, we can make a positive difference in the world.

TO THE READERS: This book is not the end, but the beginning. We want to hear from you. We want to know your stories, your insights, your questions. We want to connect with you and learn from you. We want to create a space for dialogue, feedback, and support. We want to build a network of coachable leaders who are committed to human Flourishing. Please visit becomingcoachable.com and share your thoughts with us. We look forward to hearing from you. Remember: We are in this together. Together we can change the world.

Yours in partnership,
Scott, Jacquelyn, and Marshall

The Value of Relationships

Leadership involves relationship management at every level. Relationships are the vehicle of human growth and transformation. They are the substance of our lives. Relationships have an eternal quality.

- **Embrace the value of your employees.** Employees are assets, not expenses. Treat them, and their relationships with the organization, like it.
- **Find value in the journey, not just the destination.** Flourishing is not about the end product. Because it embraces the value of relationships, it's about being, and living, in the present moment.
- **Be open to the possibility of Flourishing.** The spread of Flourishing is unpredictable. It may take hold anywhere. Flourishing is not merely additive; its effects are exponential.

It's an exciting time to be a leader. Your growth as a leader has a chance to change not only you, but also the people and the world around you.

THE SOURCES

Peter Bregman is recognized by Thinkers50 as one of the top coaches globally. He coaches C-level executives to become exceptional leaders and great human beings. He developed the Big Arrow process, which aligns teams to accomplish an organization's most important work. Peter is a contributor to sixteen books and author of five books, most recently *You Can Change Other People: The Four Steps to Help Your Colleagues, Employees—Even Family—Up Their Game.*

Alisa Cohn is an authority on leading start-ups. She is the author of *From Start-Up to Grown-Up* and the creator of a podcast of the same name. She is the executive coach for the incubator program at Cornell Tech. A frequent guest lecturer at Harvard University, Cornell University, and The US Naval War College, she regularly contributes to *Harvard Business Review, FastCompany, Inc.,* and *Forbes.*

Gene Early, PhD, is a thought leader and strategic advisor, experienced at getting to the core of individual, interpersonal, and organizational issues quickly and ecologically. Previously he was cofounder of Genomic Health, a Silicon Valley life sciences company. In addition, he has been the vice-chancellor of operations at the University of the Nations-Kona (Hawaii) and cofounded the first Neuro-Linguistic Programming (NLP) training institute in Europe.

Jennifer Goldman-Wetzler, PhD, is a leading expert on conflict and organizational psychology. Jennifer helps CEOs and their teams achieve optimal organizational health and growth. She teaches in the Department of Organization and Leadership at Columbia University and was previously a facilitator at the Program on Negotiation at Harvard Law School. Her books include *Optimal Outcomes: Free Yourself from Conflict at Work, at Home, and in Life*.

Sally Helgesen is an expert on women and leadership and the author of several seminal books on that topic. In addition to her coaching, she has delivered workshops and keynotes to organizations around the world for thirty years. Sally is a contributing editor for *Strategy+Business*. Along with Marshall Goldsmith, Sally is the coauthor of the popular book *How Women Rise: Break the 12 Habits Holding You Back from Your Next Raise, Promotion, or Job*.

Whitney Johnson is the CEO of Disruption Advisors, a leadership development company. An award-winning Wall Street analyst, Johnson was named by Thinkers50 as one of the top ten leading business thinkers in 2021, a top 200 female founder by *Inc. Magazine* in 2023, and in 2020, she was a Top Voice on LinkedIn where she has 1.8 million followers. She is the *Wall*

Street Journal bestselling author of *Smart Growth*, and hosts the popular *Disrupt Yourself* podcast.

Hubert Joly is a senior lecturer at Harvard Business School, the bestselling author of *The Heart of Business*, and the former Chairman and CEO of Best Buy. During his time there, customer satisfaction and employee engagement increased dramatically, the company's carbon footprint decreased by more than 50 percent, and Best Buy's share price rose from a low of $11 to now more than $100. Hubert is also a board member of Johnson & Johnson and Ralph Lauren Corporation.

Carol Kauffman, PhD, is on the faculty at McLean Hospital/Harvard Medical School where she founded the Institute of Coaching (IOC). She also launched the Coaching Conference at Harvard and the IOC Leadership Forum. She is the founding editor in chief of an academic journal about coaching. Her latest book, written with David Noble, is *Real-Time Leadership: Find Your Winning Move When the Stakes Are High*.

Alex Lazarus works with leaders and leadership teams around the world, enabling personal and organizational transformation through coaching, training, and cutting-edge leadership diagnostics. She is also global ambassador and senior leadership advisor for Global Leaders in Law. Previously she served as a marketing executive for the Walt Disney Company, Fox Entertainment, and Virgin Entertainment Group.

Michelle Tillis Lederman spent more than a decade as a financial executive before beginning her career as an executive coach and trainer. She was named by Forbes as one of the Top 25 Networking Experts. She has been a communications professor at New York University's Stern School of Business and a featured faculty for Lehigh University Executive Education. Michelle is an international speaker and the author of four books, most recently *The Connector's Advantage: 7 Mindsets to Grow Your Influence and Impact*.

Sharon Melnick, PhD, is an authority on women's leadership, advancement, and power, which she researched over a decade at Harvard Medical School. A sought-after coach and speaker, her approaches are field tested by leaders at seventy-five Fortune 500 companies and hundreds of conferences worldwide, including the White House and the United Nations. Her most recent book is *In Your Power: React Less, Regain Control, Raise Others*.

Nilofer Merchant is a globally recognized management thinker. In 2013, she received the Future Thinker Award from Thinkers50, given to those most likely to influence business in theory and in practice. A long-time executive at Apple and other companies, she was responsible for shipping more than one hundred products that generated revenue of $18 billion.

Dean Miles is an executive coach with over twenty years of experience. He is a member of *Forbes'* Council of Executive Coaches and the Center for Creative Leadership, as well as a fellow at the Institute of Coaching at McLean/Harvard Medical School.

Alan Mulally is the former CEO of Ford and Boeing Commercial Airplanes, and has been named #3 on *Fortune's* "World's Greatest

Leaders." Alan is well-known and recognized for his "Working Together" Leadership and Management System, including the tool kit "Culture of Love by Design" that he uses to create value for all stakeholders and the greater good worldwide.

David Noble is an executive coach, leadership advisory, and strategy consultant. He is a senior advisor to Egon Zehnder and to the Institute of Coaching. He was previously head of Asia Pacific for Oliver Wyman, global head of financial services at Kearney, a managing director at Morgan Stanley, and a senior vice president at RBC. He is coauthor, with Carol Kauffman, of *Real-Time Leadership: Find Your Winning Moves When the Stakes Are High*.

Beth Polish has many years of executive and entrepreneurial experience that informs her coaching. She was founding COO/CFO of iVillage, CFO of Goldman Sachs Ventures, and president of Dreamlife, cofounded with Anthony Robbins. As Corporate SVP she founded and directed Hearst Corporate Innovation. She has taught entrepreneurship intensives at NYU and been a featured speaker at the Women's Leadership Exchange, the Stockholm School of Economics, and many others.

Prakash Raman serves as a coach to CEOs and C-suite leaders around the globe at some of Silicon Valley's most elite companies going through hypergrowth. He led Executive Development at LinkedIn and facilitated the Leading with Mindfulness and Compassion class at the Stanford Graduate School of Business. As a tennis player, Prakash was ranked top five in the United States and number one in Texas for a record five years straight.

John Reed, PhD, is a top executive coach and trusted advisor to senior leaders and a leading advocate for stronger standards and competencies for practicing coaches to professionalize the industry. He serves as an editorial board member of the *Consulting Psychology Journal*, board member and consulting editor for the Society of Psychologists in Leadership, and a founding fellow and contributing author at the Institute of Coaching at McLean Hospital/Harvard Medical School. His latest book is *Pinpointing Excellence: Succeed with Great Executive Coaching and Steer Clear of the Rest*.

Sanyin Siang coaches and advises CEOs and their successors through the different stages of the CEO life cycle and enables them to scale and transform their companies by focusing on team dynamics. She is an investor, social media influencer, author, and a Duke University professor. She authors the Coaching Column for *MIT Sloan Management Review* and has been featured in *Wall Street Journal*, *Harvard Business Review*, *New York Times*, *Fortune*, and *Economic Times of India*.

Mike Sursock is a senior advisor at BPEA EQT. Previously, he was the managing director, chief talent officer, and head of the operations group, in which he supported investments across the group's portfolio companies pre- and post-investment. Mike previously was CEO of KKR Capstone Asia, and a vice president at Motorola. Leading up to that, Mike worked for Mars Incorporated for 20 years, most recently as president and general manager of China, leading a team devising and implementing broad-based strategies which resulted in growing market share to 60 percent of the China market. Today Mike serves as a coach and advisor to companies and leaders undergoing times of major change and growth.

Bonita Thompson, EdD, is a leading executive coach with a deep subject matter expertise in collaboration and education. She is a bestselling coauthor of *Admired: 21 Ways to Double Your Value*. Bonita has served as a senior human resources executive for global corporations and for twenty-five years was an HR innovator for six major firms: Bank of America, Genentech, Levi Strauss, Pacific Telesis, Varian, and Catellus.

Mark C. Thompson is the chairman of the Chief Executive Alliance, a partnership with the Nasdaq Center for Board Excellence. Mark served as chief of staff to founder Charles 'Chuck' Schwab during the IPO, then as his chief customer experience officer and producer of Schwab.com. Mark created the CEO Succession Readiness initiative at Stanford University and was cofounding advisor to Richard Branson's Entrepreneurship Center at Virgin. *Forbes* recognized Mark on its "Midas Touch" list of venture investors in iconic companies including Pinterest, Lyft, and Meta. Mark was founding chairman of start-ups acquired by Apple, HP, and Allstate. His books include *Success Built to Last: Creating a Life That Matters*.

Caroline Webb is a senior advisor to McKinsey & Company, where she was previously a partner and cofounded the firm's leadership practice. She also worked as an economist at the Bank of England. She is a founding fellow of the Institute of Coaching and on the advisory boards of Ethical Systems and the Constructive Dialogue Institute. A frequent contributor to

Harvard Business Review, Caroline is the author of *How to Have a Good Day: Harness the Power of Behavioral Science to Transform Your Working Life.*

ABOUT THE AUTHORS

Scott Osman is the founder and CEO of the 100 Coaches Agency, an organization designed to amplify the collective impact of the world's most iconic leadership thinkers and executive coaches. He is the codesigner of the 100 Coaches Agency's proprietary curation process and the company's relationship-first philosophy. In his role as CEO, he establishes the vision for the company, leads partnerships and business development, and serves as a critical pillar of the 100 Coaches Community, which he cofounded with Marshall Goldsmith in 2016. He is the cofounder of Methods by 100 Coaches, the online learning platform.

Jacquelyn Lane is the president of the 100 Coaches Agency and codesigner of their proprietary curation process and relationship-first philosophy. She has been with the agency since its founding and is a critical pillar of the 100 Coaches Community. Jacquelyn comes to the world of executive coaching naturally through her lifelong commitment to improving the lives of all people by elevating the quality of leadership. Previously, she held various roles in the energy industry during which time she developed deep insights into the perils and privileges of leadership.

Marshall Goldsmith is the founder of the Marshall Goldsmith Group and 100 Coaches. The inaugural winner of the Lifetime Achievement Award by the Institute of Coaching at Harvard Medical School and a Thinkers50 Management Hall of Fame inductee, he is also a professor of management at the Dartmouth Tuck School of Business and a board member for the Peter Drucker Foundation. He received his PhD from the UCLA Anderson School of Management. In his coaching practice, he has advised more than 200 major CEOs and their management teams. Marshall is the author or editor of more than thirty-five books, including *What Got You Here Won't Get You There*. His most recent book, written with Mark Reiter, is *The Earned Life: Lose Regret, Choose Fulfillment*.

ACKNOWLEDGMENTS

We've read books in general and business books in particular for years and always marveled at the extensive appreciation and recognition offered in the acknowledgments section. We marvel no more. Having run the gauntlet of writing a book, we understand that it takes a village to raise us throughout our lives, teach us and inform our thinking, and contribute at various critical junctures along the way. Each member of the village deserves recognition. About a year ago, we had an epiphany that relationships were the most essential part of our lives and that if we put relationships first, the rest (including transactions) would follow. That has proven to be a prescient understanding and has changed our lives, as well as the lives of everyone around us. We will be sharing our acknowledgments through this powerful lens of the relationship. We hope you find it as inspiring as we have.

SCOTT:

In the world of essential relationships, it is hard to overstate the importance of our relationship with Marshall. Marshall is enigmatic—one moment offering sage advice, the next providing hard-to-swallow instruction followed by a playful story and uproarious laughter. Over the past eight years, I have been in fluid collaboration with Marshall creating the MG100, which became the 100 Coaches community and then spawned the 100 Coaches Agency, where Jacquelyn joined me three years ago. I have had a front-row seat to the life of Marshall during that time, and I can attest to the following: Marshall makes the lives of millions—perhaps tens or hundreds of millions—better. He does this through his books, his speaking tours (they would make Bono blush because they are so exhaustive), and his coaching. I have personally witnessed the profound changes that come about because of Marshall's wisdom and advice. But his secret sauce is his love for his clients and the people around him, and this is truly the vehicle through which he transforms lives. His work has reminded us of the power we each have to improve the lives of those around us and inspired us to reach further in Part Three of this book. Simply put, we have written this book as an articulation of Marshall's legacy through the lens and filter of our experience. Suffice it to say, our lives are forever changed by having known Marshall, and we remain grateful, full of wonder and love, and look forward to many years of playfulness to follow.

JACQUELYN:

The 100 Coaches community has been a nurturing fountain of conversation, inspiration, and camaraderie since its founding in December 2016. The group imprinted the generosity that Marshall offered, which Peter Drucker and Frances Hesselbein had shown him, and passed it on from member to member ever since. The group was an extraordinary source of ideas and feed-back for this book which we began talking about over three years ago in some form. So many members provided crucial insights and made substantial contributions to our thinking. There are over 20 members who are listed as direct sources—they were explicitly interviewed for the book or made other significant contributions. But this book was really created by the genius of the collective. We drew deeply from the well of this eclectic mix of exceptional individuals who we are fortunate enough to call our friends. At the risk of not remembering everyone, we would like to call out the following people who made specific contributions or provided the kind of support not recognized in the text. How do we begin to acknowledge what it means to be in conversation with the likes of Martin Lindstrom, Whitney Johnson, Sanyin Siang, Dr. Jim Kim, Mike Sursock, Alex Osterwalder, Chester Elton, Sally Helgesen, Nankhonde Kasonde-van den Broek, Hubert Joly, Ayse Birsel, Peter Bregman, Srikumar Rao, Feyzi Fatehi, and Harry Kraemer. Knowing that even this long list is not exhaustive, we cannot forget to name Dorie Clark, Alisa Cohn, Sharon Melnick, Bev Wright, John Reed, Morag Barrett, Connie Dieken, Beth Polish, Bill Carrier, John Sviokla, Prakash Raman, Doug Guthrie, Bonita Thompson, Tal Ben Shahar, Michelle Johnston, Michelle Tillis Lederman, Noémie Le Pertel, Mort Aaronson, Jennifer Goldman-Wetzler, Julie Carrier, Bruce Kasanoff, Mark Reiter, Alexi Robichaux, Damian Vaughn, Brian Underhill, Alex Pascal, Caroline Webb, Jim Citrin, Erica Dhawan, Amy Edmondson, Asheesh Advani, Dacher Keltner, Tom Kolditz, Robert Glazer, Sonia Marciano, Sandy Ogg, Liz Wiseman, Rita McGrath, and Hortense le Gentil. And we'd like to remember the three beloved members of our community whom we lost this year, but who continue to inspire us through their memory: Frances Hesselbein, Chris Coffey, and David Peterson.

SCOTT:

I started developing the idea for 100 Coaches Agency in January 2018 and incorporated it in September 2020. Jacquelyn was formidable employee number two. But we only really became who we are today when we had our offsite in July of 2022 when we realized we were a relationship-first company. So we decided that if we were to be relationship-first, we should have a Chief Relationship Officer. The first person we discussed the idea with was Andy Martiniello, whom we met through Alex Oster-walder, our close friend and world changer at Strategyzer. After hearing what we were looking for, Andy simply said, "I think I'm the person for that job." And he is. His collaboration has broadened our view of the world and what it means to be a company that truly measures success in terms of the quality of our relationships rather than in terms of transactions. We were also fortunate enough to attract the exceptional talent of Niya Abdulkadir, who we were lucky enough to have with us before she was lured away by McKinsey, where we know she will thrive. Her impact on us during those six months was massive, and we are grateful to call her our collaborator and friend. Janice Gallen arrived soon after Niya. Janice is one of the most amazing people we have ever met because she is able to be both steadfast and flexible, collaborative and independent, structured and free-flowing. No matter the person or task, Janice is an effervescent presence while determinedly creating solutions. We all have so much to learn from Janice and are excited to watch her grow with us. Patrick is our newest team member, and his talent was felt immediately as he has a magic ability to make the complex simple and create solid structures out of thin air. He's an amazing problem solver and collaborator while also never being far from laughter. We are building a new kind of company that puts our relationships first, meaning we have to take care of ourselves, each other, our clients, our families, and the planet. We will explore this more in the future, and we wanted to acknowledge each of these people who supported the book's creation and the world we are currently inhabiting.

JACQUELYN:
We would also like to express our gratitude to the people our coaches coach. We consider ourselves to be in a meta-meta business—we support the coaches who support the leaders who enact real change in the lives of the people they lead and love. We firmly believe that this is the way we will create human Flourishing, and while we certainly are excited to do our part, we recognize who is on the front lines. The real heroes are the leaders we have the privilege to work with, from whom we learn with each interaction. We marvel at what they accomplish, and are proud to share their stories throughout this book. We cannot begin to mention them all, and so we will not even try to mention any of them. But know this: We see them, we honor the work they do, and we are in awe of the difference they create in the world and in the lives of those they love and lead. We hope they will read this book, recognizing their own voices within its pages, understanding that their inspiration and contributions were the essential elements that brought this work to life. We would be remiss if we did not give special thanks to Mark C. Thompson, who, in addition to writing the foreword, has been an amazing coach, mentor, and guide from the beginning of the 100 Coaches journey. He sets the bar high and supports our efforts to exceed it.

SCOTT:

We are forever grateful to those we love and who love us for providing the support and space to write the book. They also inspire us and teach us every day for all the years of our lives and for the years to come. Allegra illuminates my life with joy and laughter, dancing and delight. She creates a world of wonder for me and many others every day.

I want to specifically express my gratitude to my greatest teachers, my children Jake and Lily, whose lives are examples and inspirations to me. Jake for his creativity and commitment to ideas and ideals. Lily for her ability to innovate, her bravery, and her determination. They know how to follow their hearts to hold me accountable with grace. They are the kind of leaders and human beings I aspire to be. I am forever in their debt. I am grateful to my parents, Harley and Stephen, who have loved me and taught me to love every day of my life. There is no more fortunate child than me to have parents like them. I am deeply grateful for my sister Jamie and brother Bart, who are exceptional individuals I admire greatly and provide me with an incredible foundation of support, knowing they are always there. And to Joan and Michael who have always been there with support, laughter, and beauty.

My Romemu/Shoresh community, especially Larry/Shelly, Caren/Arthur, Angie/Norman, Marc/Karyn, Caroline/Rick, Alan, Steve/Marcia, and Karen/Peter who nourish me with their love and inspiration. And to the 100 Coaches community, which is like the Garden of Eden, creating bounty beyond imagination. And to Jane Kosstrin, my extraordinary partner at the branding and design firm Doublespace, who has taught me how to see, create, and communicate with clarity and beauty. In November

2017, I had breakfast with Scott Malkin in London and he encouraged me to dedicate myself to building 100 Coaches. I will be forever grateful for that advice as it changed the course of my life and the lives of so many others.

In January of 2018, I sat down and imagined what 100 Coaches could become, including a community, an academy, an agency, and an imprint. And in the ensuing five years, it has all come to life. What I could not have imagined then, and cannot imagine without now, is having a partner like Jacquelyn to build and grow the business, the thinking, the heart, and the soul of everything we do. I am grateful for our collaboration and in awe of what she already has done and what I know she will accomplish. Through our collaboration, we are modeling the world of work we hope everyone will experience.

MARSHALL:

My life is better because of an amazing partner who holds me close and allows me to work far and wide. Lyda is my forever coach who makes sure I stay open to change and new ideas, who is always willing to take action, and who holds me accountable in a way I am always grateful for. She enables me to live an earned life. My daughter Kelly demonstrates the power of commitment and determination and inspires me to live up to my highest standards, and my son Brian teaches me how not to take life so seriously and how we can get results without a final blueprint. And my grandchildren Avery and Austin demonstrate that we are no match for the next generation who will find paths and solutions that we have not yet imagined.

And, of course, to my greatest coaches, the people I have coached, including Alan Mulally who I am still learning from, and from the late Paul Hersey, Peter Drucker, and Frances Hesslebein who each supported my growth and helped me become coachable. And I thank each and every member of the 100 Coaches community. You have each made my life better. Life, indeed, is good.

JACQUELYN:

To my incredible husband, Michael, thank you for your endless love and support. Thank you for picking up countless little tasks to allow me the time and space to dive into this project and for keeping me fed, watered, and caffeinated. Thank you for listening to me read section after section to ensure that the flow and tone landed just right. Thank you for your courageous journey into the coaching world, first as a client and later as a coach yourself. Your journey has inspired my own and brought me into the work that is my heart's calling.

Thank you to my incredible parents, Gary and Renee, whose unwavering faith in me has propelled me all my life to dream a little bigger. I'm the most blessed person I know to have your love and cheerleading. Thank you to my wonderful sisters, Rebecca and Kaitlyn, my two most precious friends. You make me laugh, inspire me, and make me feel at home anywhere.

Thank you to my many wonderful teachers along the way: John Musso, Vicki Walter, Dr. Paul Tikalsky, Dr. Karl Reid, Dr. Ashlee Ford-Versypt, Susan Jordan, Dr. Dai Morgan, Ann Olgesby, Heath DePriest, Ronald Sanchez, Heath Dieckert, Evening Galvin, and Meg Wolf. Thank you to my dearest friends who have supported and encouraged me every step of the way including Monica Valdez, Soeren Walls, Tori Bell, Savanna Robison, Chance Imhoff, Daniel Anderson, Brett Humphrey, Courtney Anderson,

Sarah Anderson, Niya Abdulkadir, Kyle Negrete, Christianne Taylor, and Meghan Kelleher, among many others. I wish I could name you all.

Thank you to this incredible 100 Coaches community—you have changed my life with your love and friendship. I consider myself the luckiest person in the world to work with and learn from the best of the best. May we always grow together. Thank you, Marshall, for creating this amazing community. Thank you for symbolically adopting me, being one of my greatest teachers and sources of joy. You encapsulate generosity. And lastly, thank you to Scott, who has become so much more than a collaborator and partner, but also a best friend. Every day we spend working together is joy upon joy—I can hardly call it work. There is no one with whom I feel more united in mission and purpose. We have come such a long way in only three years; I can hardly fathom the next three, five, or ten.

MARSHALL:
In August 2022, the 100 Coaches held its first post-pandemic annual community gathering in Nashville. On Saturday night at Belmont University in the Fisher Center for Performing Arts, we were treated to an evening of songs performed by the song-writers. They explained how the songwriting process is very collaborative—one person may have an idea for a tune, and another may have some words that fit the melody. Still, another refines and builds on the song, and by the end, it is unclear who did what because there is one voice that expresses the song. This is a perfect metaphor for this book.

SCOTT:

I began playing around with the idea for a book three years ago; the idea for the book you are holding materialized in June of 2022. I brought Stephen O'Shea in to help write a book proposal. Stephen is a writer friend I first met and collaborated with 35 years ago in Paris and whose work and writing voice I have admired ever since. We started to work on the proposal, bouncing ideas off members of the 100 Coaches community, most notably in my Wednesday Zoom group, whose regular participants include Dean Miles, Beth Polish, Andrew Novak, Evelyn Rodstein, Mark Goulston, and David Cohen. I also have to give a lot of gratitude to Mark Reiter, a brilliant writer/agent and Marshall's co-author, who, after hearing a few ideas, told me to write the book that only we could write where we had the authority to tell the story. And a thank you to Gene Early and Nilofer Merchant, my amazing coaches (really, the coaches for our entire team) for being our early sounding boards and encouragers. We drew deeply from the well of Marshall's teaching, which we were very familiar with. In September 2022, Jacquelyn and I met with Eric Schurenberg, an early member of 100 Coaches and the former editor-in-chief of Fast Company and Inc. Magazine, to discuss creating a 100 Coaches imprint with Amplify Publishing Group, a company he had joined. For five years, I had wanted to establish a 100 Coaches imprint but had never found the right partner.

JACQUELYN:

In October, we met with Naren Aryal of Amplify and instantly knew that Eric was right, and this was the right timing and partnership for us. We decided that this book, Becoming Coachable, would be the first book for the imprint and set a very aggressive timeline for publishing. We reviewed the book proposal that Stephen had drafted and, in late November, decided to bring in veteran Inc. writer Leigh Buchanan to take the handoff and begin researching the hypothesis we had constructed. Starting in January, Leigh did a brilliant job of gathering information and interviewing close to two dozen of the top coaches in the world and, by the end of February, had written the first draft of the manuscript that provided the basis for this book.

Scott and I felt there was something missing, and we brought Stephen back into the writing process and added Nilofer Merchant to support with broad strategic thinking about what we wanted to say. During this time, Part Three was contemplated, the conversations were had, and the section was written. Our thinking was further reinforced and refined through conversations with Nilofer Merchant, Andy Martiniello, and Stephen O'Shea over several days in New York—a true gathering of the minds. Additionally, we had some wonderful readers and other thinking partners who shared invaluable perspectives and contributions, including Sudhir Venkatesh, Dean Miles, Beth Polish, Alan Mulally, and Sarah McArthur.

SCOTT:
I want to pause this narrative and call out Naren and Nina Spahn, who, at this point, could have been angry about missed deadlines and changing goals but instead were massively supportive and encouraging. They shared our vision completely, and committed to supporting it in every way they could. Nina would become an important voice in the narrative; she was our unofficial editor who rolled up her sleeves, challenged our thinking, made additions where needed, and kept us honest.

Marshall, Jacquelyn, and I spent many hours walking in malls discussing the book, coaching, and what it takes to become coachable. Marshall's fingerprints are all over the book, including on the meta-level of providing us with ideas and inspiration. We each contributed our writing, our stories, and our hearts to this work, which brought the manuscript to life.

In what we thought would be the final days and what became the final weeks, Jacquelyn gave the book the final layers of varnish to fully realize the level of finish we aspired to. Her commitment to excellence and dedication to the reader would not allow her to let go until the book was ready. Together, she and Nina spent many late nights sweating the details. In every possible way, Jacquelyn is the most perfect partner imaginable, and this book and the world I currently inhabit would not be possible without her.

CHORUS:

Like a team of songwriters, it is hard to know who said what by the end, except where noted. More importantly, like the Nashville songwriters, all of us—Eric, Naren, Leigh, Stephen, Nilofer, Andy, Nina, Marshall, Jacquelyn, and Scott—have written in one voice that speaks clearly to you, the reader, and shares what we consider to be one of the most meaningful messages you can hear.

With love, gratitude, and wonder,
Scott, Jacquelyn, and Marshall

FURTHER READING

Bregman, Peter. *Leading with Emotional Courage How to Have Hard Conversations, Create Accountability, and Inspire Action on Your Most Important Work*. Wiley, 2018.

Cohn, Alisa. *From Start-Up to Grown-Up: Grow Your Leadership to Grow Your Business*. Kogan Page, 2021.

Gist, Marilyn, and Alan Mulally. *The Extraordinary Power of Leader Humility: Thriving Organizations—Great Results*. Berrett-Koehler Publishers, 2020.

Goldman-Wetzler, Jennifer. *Optimal Outcomes: Free Yourself from Conflict at Work, at Home, and in Life*. Harper Business, an Imprint of HarperCollins Publishers, 2020.

Goldsmith, Marshall, and Alan Mulally. "Working Together Webinar with Alan Mulally." YouTube. Video. December 7, 2020. www.youtube.com/watch?v=QN6IyAM3bGE.

Goldsmith, Marshall, and Mark Reiter. *Triggers: Creating Behavior That Lasts—Becoming the Person You Want to Be*. Currency, 2015.

Goldsmith, Marshall, and Mark Reiter. *What Got You Here Won't Get You There: How Successful People Become Even More Successful!* Hachette Books, an Imprint of Hachette Books, 2015.

Goldsmith, Marshall, et al. *Lessons from Leaders Volume 1: Practical Lessons for a Lifetime of Leadership*. Leadership Studies, Inc., 2021.

Helgesen, Sally, and Marshall Goldsmith. *How Women Rise: Break the 12 Habits Holding You Back*. Random House Business, 2019.

Helgesen, Sally. *Rising Together: How We Can Bridge Divides and Create a More Inclusive Workplace*. Hachette Go Books, 2023.

Hesselbein, Frances, et al. *Work Is Love Made Visible: a Collection of Essays about the Power of Finding Your Purpose from the World's Greatest Thought Leaders*. Wiley, 2018.

Hoffman, Bryce G. *American Icon: Alan Mulally and the Fight to Save Ford Motor Company*. Crown Business, 2012.

Johnson, Whitney. *Smart Growth: How to Grow Your People to Grow Your Company*. Harvard Business Review Press, 2022.

Lederman, Michelle Tillis. *The Connector's Advantage: 7 Mindsets to Grow Your Influence and Impact*. Page Two, 2019.

Melnick, Sharon. *In Your Power: React Less, Regain Control, Raise Others*. Wiley, 2022.

Merchant, Nilofer. *The Power of Onlyness: Make Your Wild Ideas Mighty Enough to Dent the World*. Viking, 2017.

Mulally, Alan, and Sarah McArthur. "A Conversation with Alan Mulally about His 'Working Together'© Strategic, Operational, And Stakeholder-Centered Management System." *Leader to Leader* (2022): pp. 7–14. https://doi.org/10.1002/ltl.20628.

Noble, David, and Carol Kauffman. *Real-Time Leadership: Find Your Winning Moves When the Stakes Are High*. Harvard Business Review Press, 2023.

Porras, Jerry I., et al. *Success Built to Last: Creating a Life That Matters*. Wharton School Pub. 2006.

Sabbagh, Karl. *Twenty-First Century Jet: The Making and Marketing of the Boeing 777*. Scribner, 1996.

Siang, Sanyin. *The Launch Book: 50 Ways To Launch Your Idea, Business Or Next Career*. LID Publishing, 2017.

Webb, Caroline. *How to Have a Good Day: Harness the Power of Behavioral Science to Transform Your Working Life*. Currency, 2016.

ENDNOTES

1   Marshall Goldsmith and Mark Reiter, *What Got You Here Won't Get You There: How Successful People Become Even More Successful!* (Profile Books, 2012).

2   Joan Shafer, Adam Bryant, and David Reimer, "Revealing leaders' blind spots," *Strategy+Business*, April 29, 2020, https://www.strategy-business.com/article/Revealing-leaders-blind-spots.

3   Marian F. MacDorman, Marie Thoma, Eugene Declcerq, and Elizabeth A. Howell, "Racial and Ethnic Disparities in Maternal Mortality in the United States Using Enhanced Vital Records, 2016-2017," *American Journal of Public Health* 111, no. 9, (April 2021): pp. 1673–1681, https://doi.org/10.2105/ajph.2021.306375.

4   World Bank Group, "Data: Poverty," *World Bank Open Data*, https://data.worldbank.org/topic/poverty?end=2017&start=2012.

5   Robert Hendrickson, *The Facts on File Encyclopedia of Word and Phrase Origins*, fourth edition, (Facts On File, 2008).

6   Josh Wilson, "Oprah Winfrey, Hugh Jackman, And Other Celebrities Recommend Coaching As A Necessity for Success," *Forbes*, September 24, 2022, www.forbes.com/sites/joshwilson/2022/09/24/oprah-winfrey-hugh-jackman-and-other-celebrities-recommend-coaching-as-a-necessity-for-success/?sh=11205a7f7869.

7   Jeffrey P. Bezos, "1997 Letter to Shareholders," Amazon, 1997, https://www.sec.gov/Archives/edgar/data/1018724/000119312516530910/d168744dex991.htm.

8   Merrill C. Anderson, PhD, "Executive Briefing: Case Study on the Return on Investment of Executive Coaching," MetrixGlobal, November 2, 2001.

9   Amy Gallo, "How to Get Feedback When You're the Boss," *Harvard Business Review,* May 15, 2012, https://hbr.org/2012/05/how-to-get-feedback-when-youre.

10 Marshall Goldsmith and Howard Morgan, "Leadership Is a Contact Sport: The 'Follow-up Factor' in Management Development," *Strategy+Business,* August 25, 2004, https://www.strategy-business.com/article/04307.

11 Ben Laker, "Why Modern Executives Are More Susceptible to Hubris Than Ever," *MIT Sloan Management Review,* August 17, 2021, https://sloanreview.mit.edu/article/why-modern-executives-are-more-susceptible-to-hubris-than-ever/.

12 Alex Gray, "Read this: how our brains are wired to respond to confident people," World Economic Forum, March 15, 2017, https://www.weforum.org/agenda/2017/03/read-this-how-our-brains-are-wired-to-respond-to-confident-people/.

13 Inch, "Debate: Is Change Always a Good Thing," Ineos.com, Rich Newman quote, 2015, https://www.ineos.com/inch-magazine/articles/issue-8/debate-is-change-always-a-good-thing/.

14 Sihame Benmira and Moyosolu Agboola, "Evolution of leadership theory," *BMJ Leader* 5, no. 1 (2021): 3–5. https://bmjleader.bmj.com/content/5/1/3.

15 Kurt Lewin, "Patterns of aggressive behavior in experimentally created 'social climates,'" *The complete social scientist: A Kurt Lewin reader* (1999): pp. 227–250, https://doi.org/10.1037/10319-008, https://tu-dresden.de/mn/psychologie/ipep/lehrlern/ressourcen/dateien/lehre/lehramt/lehrveranstaltungen/Lehrer_Schueler_Interaktion_SS_2011/Lewin_1939_original.pdf?lang=en.

16 John Gerzema and Michael D'Antonio, *The Athena Doctrine: How Women (And The Men Who Think Like Them) Will Rule the Future* (San Francisco: Jossey-Bass): p. 3.

17 Glennon Doyle, "Five Criticism Survival Strategies," *We Can Do Hard Things with Glennon Doyle, Apple Podcasts*, February 9, 2023, podcasts.apple.com/us/podcast/five-criticism-survival-strategies/id1564530722?i=1000598975841.

18 Mark R. Leary, "The Psychology of Intellectual Humility," John Templeton Foundation, https://www.templeton.org/wp-content/uploads/2018/11/Intellectual-Humility-Leary-FullLength-Final.pdf.

19 Adam Grant, "Does intrinsic motivation fuel the prosocial fire? Motivational synergy in predicting persistence, performance, and productivity," *Journal of Applied Psychology* 93, no. 1 (2008): 48–58, https://doi.org/10.1037/0021-9010.93.1.48.

20 Yoon Jik Cho and James L. Perry, "Intrinsic Motivation and Employee Attitudes: Role of Managerial Trustworthiness, Goal Directedness, and Extrinsic Reward Expectancy," *Review of Public Personnel Administration* 32, no. 4 (2012): 382–406, https://doi.org/10.1177/0734371X11421495.

21 R.F. Baumeister, E. Bratslavsky, M. Muraven, and D.M. Tice, "Ego depletion: Is the active self a limited resource?" *Journal of Personality and Social Psychology* 74, no. 5 (May 1998): pp. 1252–1265.

22 Ailsa Chang and Daniel Gilbert, "Why Climate Change Threats Don't Trigger An Immediate Response From Human Brains," *All Things Considered*, NPR, December 12, 2019, https://www.npr.org/2019/12/12/787552712/why-climate-change-threats-dont-trigger-an-immediate-response-from-human-brains.

23 Faiz Siddiqui and Jeremy B. Merrill, "Musk issues ultimatum to staff: Commit to 'hardcore' Twitter or take severance," *Washington Post*, November 16, 2022, https://www.washingtonpost.com/technology/2022/11/16/musk-twitter-email-ultimatum-termination/.

24 Esther Crawford tweet: "When your team is pushing round the clock to make deadlines sometimes you #SleepWhereYouWork" (@esthercrawford), https://twitter.com/esthercrawford/status/1587709705488830464.

25 Dianela Perdomo, "Human flourishing: Could a philosophical concept impact health?" *Biomedical Odyssey*, October 28, 2021, https://biomedicalodyssey.blogs.hopkinsmedicine.org/2021/10/human-flourishing-could-a-philosophical-concept-impact-health/#:~:text=Aristotelian%20Flourishing&text=In%20ancient%20Greece%2C%20circa%20300.